Family-Friendly Biking

in

New Jersey and Eastern Pennsylvania

Family-Friendly Biking

in

New Jersey and Eastern Pennsylvania

DIANE GOODSPEED

RUTGERS UNIVERSITY PRESS

NEW BRUNSWICK, NEW JERSEY, AND LONDON

Fourth paperback printing, 2011

Library of Congress Cataloging-in-Publication Data

Goodspeed, Diane, 1962–
    Family-friendly biking in New Jersey and Eastern Pennsylvania / Diane
Goodspeed.
        p. cm.
    1. Bicycle touring—New Jersey—Guidebooks. 2. Bicycle touring—
Pennsylvania—Guidebooks. 3. Family recreation—New Jersey—Guidebooks.
4. Family recreation—Pennsylvania—Guidebooks. 5. New Jersey—
Guidebooks. 6. Pennsylvania—Guidebooks. I. Title.
    GV1045.5.G66 2005
    796.6′4—dc22

                                                2004020837

A British Cataloging-in-Publication record for this book is available from the
British Library

Manufactured in the United States of America

Kevin and Kathleen
Don't ever get too old for snoop loops.

Contents

Family-Friendly Biking

in

New Jersey and Eastern Pennsylvania

.

Introduction

For several years after we had kids, we gave up bike riding. While biking was still our favorite hobby, biking on the road with kids did not seem safe, and biking across a mountain was just plain impossible—maybe even insane. So we spent several years biking around, and around, and around our neighborhood. Eventually, the kids got older, we got desperate, and I began searching for trails other than road routes. What I found were trails with descriptions like "leg-burning gravel climbs" or "extra gnarly through deep sand" or "a great stump jumper." Are these bike trails or goat paths? This was not what I wanted to ride with a two-year-old toddler in a bike seat . . . even if my thrill-seeking daughter would have been delighted!

So our quest began—to find bike trails suitable and fun for the entire family. Fortunately, once we started (and finally convinced friends that no road, no matter how quiet and quaint, is safe for a five-year-old), we found a few trails that eventually lead to more trails. We were struck immediately by how few families used these trails—wonders that they are—so I decided to write this book.

Trails described here are not on roads and do not cross mountains! In fact, we rode every trail with Kevin, who is seven and generally just barely visible on the trail ahead of us, and Kathleen, who at four rides in a bike seat on my bike, maintaining a running commentary for the duration of the trip (yeah, really).

Once we became convinced that family biking was possible (and might even be fun), we found three excellent sources for family-friendly bike trails. First, we tapped into the Rails-to-Trails Conservancy, a nonprofit organization that sponsors and guides the conversion of old railroad lines into multi-use trails. Rail-trails are "multi-purpose, public paths that encourage outdoor recreation, promote fitness, serve as historic and conservation corridors and create greenways through developed areas." Across the country, there are over a thousand rail-trails, covering almost 11,000 miles, and new trails are converted every year. Rail-trails are ideal for family biking because they are typically flat, wide, and usually have a packed cinder surface. For more information on rail-trails, go to www.railtrails.org or call 202-331-9696.

Second, we began exploring the remaining canal systems. Local organizations, through sheer hard work, have restored many of the towpaths in New Jersey and Pennsylvania. Although not all are continuous, there are many sections open for biking. Finally, we asked everyone with a bike and kids where they ride. Biking families provided us with some great rides in New Jersey and eastern Pennsylvania parks.

After we heard or read about a potential trail, we rode the trail. This is a lot easier said than done due to phantom trailheads, nonexistent parking areas, supposed smooth trails with deadly ruts and rocks, and documented flat trails with a few undocumented killer hills. There were also a few trails that disappeared into parking areas, strip malls, and backyards. Some of our biggest challenges were on the 30-mile-long towpaths and rail-trails. We drove or biked long sections looking for the ones best suited to biking with children.

After riding the trails or trail sections to find the family-friendly ones, I conducted what my kids refer to as "snoop loops." Biking with young kids is not simply a matter of throwing the bikes and kids in the car. Oh, no! Many of our early trips were destroyed by a lack of restrooms or French fries! Decades ago (okay, maybe it was just a few years), we rode 10 or 15 miles before stopping for a water break, and a great ride was based on how far we got before exhaustion or a setting sun turned us for home. Today we ride in terms of "ten more trees before you stop." All right, I exaggerate . . . a bit. But where on a mountain bike does the diaper bag go?

So what we do is investigate the area around the bike trail. We search for all the parking areas, restaurants, parks, attractions, and good places to stop. My kids also check out every single restroom (sometimes twice, just to be sure) on every bike route. I also research the history of the surrounding area, particularly for the rail-trails and canal towpaths. So when your kids ask, "What's that?" you have an answer. My goal is to provide you with all the details and information necessary to bike as a family. If there are no restrooms, I tell you. If there are restrooms, I tell you where so you can find them—fast! If there is fun *stuff* nearby, I tell you what and where to find it. If there are multiple access points to a trail, I tell you where and at what distances. I also included rides of different lengths ranging from 2 to 12 miles, with a few that can be extended to 20-plus miles.

In addition to selecting a variety of terrains and distances, I picked trails that offer more than just a bike ride. Our kids enjoy biking more when we find a playground, stream, fishing spot, historic site, or hiking area to explore along the way. Many of our trips have also been saved by ice cream, so we located as many ice cream shops as possible along the paths or in the vicinity!

I have also included a chapter describing the trails we investigated and rejected. Trails were rejected for multiple reasons but mostly due to traffic. If it was due to trail surface conditions, please remember that conditions and situations change as trails become more popular and are better maintained by state, county, and local park officials. The reverse is also true. Trail conditions change constantly, and public parks are subject to closures due to maintenance work or planned improvements. The descriptions in this book are what we found. And, while I know you will not find a new hill on a restored towpath or a highway through the middle of a state park, you may find a washed-out section or different surface conditions. Before you go it is always wise to check for current trail conditions via the Internet or by calling the park.

Before You Go

A fun bike ride depends on a good bicycle and equipment, a little preparation, and detailed trail information. The majority of this book is dedicated to trail information, but first . . . a quick discussion of bikes, equipment, and safety.

BICYCLES AND EQUIPMENT

There are many options and choices for bikes and equipment. Furthermore, they are constantly being improved. Whether you are an experienced rider or just starting out, my recommendation is to check with your local bike store. A good bike store carries a wide range of bikes and equipment and knows what is available and what is new. And your local dealer may also be able to provide some low-cost options for the latest equipment.

BICYCLES

There are bikes for all interest levels and price ranges. For trail riding, most bike stores recommend a basic, all-terrain bike. But whatever you have or buy, every trail bike should have a water bottle holder, well-padded handgrips, and lots of reflectors.

BIKE TYPES. There are three basic bike types:

Lightweight street or racing bikes. These bikes have light frames, lots of gears, and are typically outfitted with toe clips, hand brakes, narrow seats, dropped handle bars, and very narrow, hard tires. They are best for long-distance rides on smoothly paved roads.

Mountain or all-terrain bikes. These bikes have medium-weight, sturdy frames with knobby tires. There are generally ten to eighteen gears, hand brakes, and wider seats. They are good on rough ground, like gravel, cinder, or packed dirt. An all-terrain bike is also very good on paved roads.

Motor cross or BMX bikes. These bikes have small, heavy-duty frames, raised handlebars, heavy-tread tires, and a rear foot brake. They are used primarily for mountain biking, dirt racing, and trick riding.

BIKE SIZE. A bike that is the wrong size can be downright dangerous. Your bike shop fitted you with the right bike when you bought it. Children, however, grow constantly. To ensure the right fit for children, check the following every six months or so.

Frame size. Place the child's feet on either side of the bike's crossbar. There should be two to three inches of clearance between the child and crossbar.

Seat height. Sit child on seat. The child should be able to balance the bike without difficulty. A slight lean is fine but the bike must be stable. Your child should also have only a slight bend in the leg with a foot on the pedal at the bottom of the rotation. Too much knee bending tires the leg muscles. A dead giveaway . . . when their knees touch their elbows as they pedal, it is time to raise the seat or buy a bigger bike!

Handlebars. Grips should be just above seat level. The seat on an all-terrain or mountain bike should *never* be above the handlebars.

BIKE CARRIERS

Carrier choice is largely dependent on your vehicle size and type and the number of bikes you are taking. Over the last four years, we used a roof rack, a rear van carrier, and a hitch carrier. All work well.

Our choice was dictated by which type of child carrier we had for our daughter. With every bike carrier, we find it helpful to have several extra bungee cords on hand to ensure a snug hold. An extra-long bike chain to lock bikes onto the car is also useful.

CHILD CARRIERS

There are three main choices: bike seat, cart, or a tandem attachment. Your choice is dependent on the age, size, and riding ability of your child. No matter what choice you make, keep an eye on the weight. Remember, you are adding the carrier plus the child's weight to your own bike (or if you are really clever, your partner's bike!). Either way, with a 25-pound child and an 8-pound carrier, you are adding 33 pounds!

BIKE SEATS. There are a large number of these on the market from a range of manufacturers with an even wider price range. Most bike seats are molded plastic and have a maximum allowed weight of 40 pounds. Due to the limited leg space between seat and carrier, you should also factor in your child's size. Our son outgrew his bike seat long before he reached 40 pounds! Some basic considerations when selecting a bike seat: (1) Feet buckets should be deep enough for your child's shoe. Some have shoe straps to keep little feet inside the buckets while others have an adjustable height for longer use. (2) Harness should have three or four attachment points and should adjust easily. (3) Grab bar (if there is one) should move for easy loading and unloading. (4) Sides and seat back should be high for comfort but with an unobstructed side view. Also consider the shape and size of your child's helmet. Some seats have a molded headrest to allow for the helmet. Another consideration is whether your child's head can be supported if he/she falls asleep. (5) Spoke guards provide extra protection for little feet but do not replace a good foot bucket. (6) Make sure there is a quick-release/attach system if you must remove the seat to transport the bike. (7) The suspension should have springs to ensure a smooth ride. This is indescribably important for very young children.

CARTS. There are one-child and two-child carts. And two-child carts have either side-by-side or front-back seating. During our cart stage, we found the bike required more maintenance due to the pull and tug of the cart. Remember, helmets must be worn even in the cart. Some basic considerations when selecting a cart: (1) Backward- and forward-facing seats have several pros and cons. Forward-facing seats allow kids to see you, but the trail view is limited. Make sure the side view is not obstructed. A backward-facing seat provides a better view of the trail and surroundings, but you cannot see the child! (2) Your choice of construction material is either an aluminum frame or molded plastic. (3) A waterproof cover and/or rain-fly is an absolute must. A mesh screen is useful to keep sun exposure to a minimum. (4) The harness should be a three- or four-point system with adjustable straps. (5) The bike connector should allow the cart to stay upright even if the bike falls over, or the connection should be made at multiple points on the bike to provide maximum stability. (6) Weight allowed for carts can range from 25 to 75 pounds. Remember to include children and gear weight. (7) Transporting a cart can be difficult. Some have quick-release tires and folding frames for easy storage and transport. (8) Some carts also provide a storage area for gear.

TANDEM ATTACHMENT. This is a great option for an older child who knows how to bike but is not ready to go it alone. Sometimes referred to as a "tag-along," a tandem attachment is basically a bike—minus the front wheel—that attaches to your bike, thus converting any regular bike into a tandem. You control the speed, direction, and braking. Your child gets to "ride" and pedal (theoretically). Some basics to selecting a tandem attachment: (1) Frame should be lightweight and should fold or detach for transport and storage. (2) The connectors should allow the bike to turn. Rigid connectors make it hard to handle corners. (3) Seat height should be adjustable. Some tandems also have adjustable handlebars. (4) A splashguard or bike rack should be used on the adult bike to prevent water, dirt, and debris from hitting the child's legs.

HELMETS

New Jersey and Pennsylvania law requires all children under twelve years of age to wear a helmet when biking. The helmet must meet American National Standards Institute (ANSI), American Society for Testing and Materials (ASTM), or Snell Memorial Foundation safety standards. It should be worn flat atop the head and should fit snugly. Have your children put on their helmets and vigorously shake their heads up, down, and side-to-side. A properly fit helmet will not slide, move, or fall off. A helmet that falls off in a crash does little to protect your head! And the chinstrap should always be buckled! Use your local bike shop to get a correct fit. We budget a new helmet for the kids every year. Of course, adults should also wear helmets.

SAFETY

A pre-ride inspection and a few simple safety rules can make a huge difference in a day out biking. It is better to be cautious than sorry. Always use common sense and remember that you are ultimately responsible for your own fun and safe travels.

SAFETY GUIDELINES

- Wear lightweight, light-colored clothes in easy-to-modify layers.
- Use a pant clip or large rubber band on the right leg to keep long pants away from the bike chain.
- Wear closed-toe shoes with short or no laces. If you do wear shoes with long laces, tuck the laces into the shoes.
- Take lots of breaks, especially in hot or humid weather. Plan to double your breaks on the return.
- When passing another biker or walker, call out your passing side (e.g., "Passing left") so the individual(s) can move over. Be courteous to bikers passing you.
- Walk bikes at road crossings and cross as a group.
- When biking on loose gravel or uneven ground, teach young bikers to brake with the back brakes. Make sure they also understand how to balance on hills and/or rough trails.

- Do not ride trails at night. Plan to complete your ride before dusk, when the trail surface becomes hard to see. Deer also become a worry at dusk as they are quite good at leaping into a biker's path.
- Always yield to walkers and horseback riders. Walking bikes past horses is generally a good idea if you are not familiar with their behavior. When in doubt, ask the rider.
- Most of the trails in this book are very popular with dog walkers, most of whom are very considerate of bikers and have well-mannered dogs. If you do encounter a loose dog or one that is not under control, dismount and walk with the bike between you and the dog. Keep quiet. Stop and wait for the owner to collect the dog. Never, ever try to out-race a dog. They can be surprisingly fast when their "prey drive" is activated.
- After every ride, do a quick tick check. Most trails are wide enough to keep you away from bushes and shrubs but ticks are everywhere. Shake out jackets, brush down shirts and shorts, and comb through hair. Avoid wearing fleece. Ticks stick to it like glue!
- In the fall, wear bright colors (red, yellow, and orange) and keep in mind that hunting is allowed in wildlife management areas.
- In the unlikely event you encounter a black bear, put your bike between the bear and you and your child. Avoid direct eye contact. Make lots of noise. Move backward slowly but steadily. If the bear seems threatening, the New Jersey Division of Fish and Wildlife says to make lots of noise and to throw rocks and sticks to frighten the bear away. Please remember that bears are shy, solitary creatures that are very happy to disappear quietly into the woods when people approach. So noise is a great deterrent. If the bear hears you coming, it will graciously vacate the area.
- Pack a small plastic bag for garbage. Nearly all state and national parks and many county parks are "carry in, carry out." A word of warning . . . after several years of trail riding, my kids now try to collect *all* the garbage. We carry a really sturdy bag and argue a lot over what can be carried safely "out" on a bike!
- Use a backpack or bike pack to carry all your supplies. Make sure every bike has a water bottle.

- Consider bringing along a cell phone, camera, and a small notebook and pencil. While not essentials, they can make life easier and more fun. Also remember to carry some cash.
- Bring the following essentials on every ride: plenty of water or sports drinks, first aid kit, bike tube filler and basic repair kit, trail map, hand wipes, sunscreen, bike lock, insect repellent, and nutritious, high-energy snacks. For example, one of Kathleen's favorite parts about biking is making up the "gorp" for our rides. GORP (Good Old Raisins and Peanuts) is the traditional snack of bikers and hikers, providing energy and nutrition. Use the following basic recipe and be creative:

    1 cup dry-roasted, salted peanuts
    1 cup raisins
    1 cup plain M&Ms

    Optional in 1-cup quantities: stick pretzels, small cheese crackers, chocolate chips, butterscotch chips, granola chunks, mixed nuts instead of peanuts, dried fruit, dry cereal, or Kathleen's favorite, colored mini-marshmallows

PRE-RIDE CHECKLIST

A quick inspection of your bike and equipment can often prevent problems from occurring during a ride. A yearly overhaul from your local bike shop is also a good insurance policy.

TIRES. Check for proper inflation and good treads. Treads should not have cracks or wear spots.

BRAKES. Check for smooth, quiet operation. Well-adjusted brakes do not pull or squeak.

SEAT. Adjust for proper height. Make sure seat clips are tight and springs are rust-free.

CHAIN. Keep clean, free of rust, and oiled correctly. Chain should have half-inch leeway or give in tension.

WHEELS. Check for loose or missing spokes. Well-balanced wheels do not wobble when spun.

PEDALS. Should turn easily and not have worn treads.

CHILD SEAT. Check clips for smooth operation. They should turn easily and be rust-free. Check harness straps for fraying or excessive wear.

How to Use This Book

User Categories

Every biker (young and old) has different abilities and tolerances. Rather than provide a bump-by-bump description of each trail, ruining your own quest for adventure, I created four usage categories to help you decide which trails are best suited to your family.

YOUNG BIKER. A rider who can handle multiple surfaces, terrain variations, and longer distances.

JUNIOR BIKER. A rider with or just out of training wheels, who needs smooth pavement or well-packed cinder and mostly level terrain.

PRESCHOOLER. Preschooler or toddler in a bike seat, cart, or tandem who can handle a few bumps and longer rides.

TODDLER. Toddler or baby in a bike seat or cart who needs smooth pavement and relatively short rides.

Glossary

I use the following terms in the book to describe the trails:

out-and-back Rail-trails and canal towpaths are straight and flat, but you usually have to return by the same path. The distance stated is for the entire trip: out and then back.

loop Many of the county park trails are complete loops. The distance stated is for the full loop.

packed cinder A surface made of ground-up stone that is packed, hard. It is smooth, easy to ride on, and absorbs water without getting muddy or soft, making for a good ride even after heavy rains or in early spring after the snow melt.

packed gravel A surface made of small, crushed stone that is packed down. This is an easy surface to ride on but may be difficult under wet conditions.

ballast A surface made of large stone, typically found along railroad tracks. It is almost impossible to ride on.

single track This is a dirt or grass path with a four- to six-inch track cut in it—most likely by bikes. Single track can be difficult after heavy rains or through woods, where you run out of knee and elbow room! Single track on the towpaths is usually fine.

double track This is a dirt or grass path with two tracks cut in it—most likely by trucks or ATVs. Wider than single track with a hard packed surface, for obvious reasons, double track also provides easy riding.

MAPS AND MAP LEGEND

There is one map for each trail. Due to their length, some trail systems have multiple "rides." On these maps all the rides are shown, which means there are multiple start and end points, and detail maps are included for some of the start and end points.

Please note that the maps are *not drawn to scale* and should not be used to calculate distance. When biking for family fun, you need to know where to park and where to locate restrooms more than you need exact dimensions between every road and creek!

LEGEND. The following symbols are used on all trail maps:

P　　Parking Area

 Start of Bike Ride

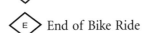 End of Bike Ride

－－－－ Bike Trail—The ride described in the chapter

.... Alternate Bike Trail—Nearby trail but not part of ride(s) described

－·－·－· Missing Trail

▬▬▬ Major Highway

——— Minor Highway or Road

✧   Point of Interest

◆   City or Town

TRAIL LOCATOR MAP

The trail number corresponds to the chapter number.

NEW JERSEY TRAILS
 1. Sussex Branch Trail
 2. Kittatinny Valley State Park
 3. Paulinskill Valley Trail
 4. Loantaka Brook Reservation
 5. Patriots' Path–Morristown
 6. Traction Line Trail
 7. Columbia Trail
 8. Black River Wildlife Management Area
 9. Liberty State Park
10. Duke Island Park
11. Landsdown Trail
12. Hoffman Park
13. Delaware & Raritan Main Canal
14. Sandy Hook National Recreation Area
15. Hartshorne Woods Park
16. Edgar Felix Bike Path
17. Manasquan Reservoir
18. Delaware & Raritan Feeder Canal
19. Cooper River Park

PENNSYLVANIA TRAILS
20. Delaware Canal
21. Tyler State Park
22. Hugh Moore Park
23. Lehigh Canal
24. McDade Trail

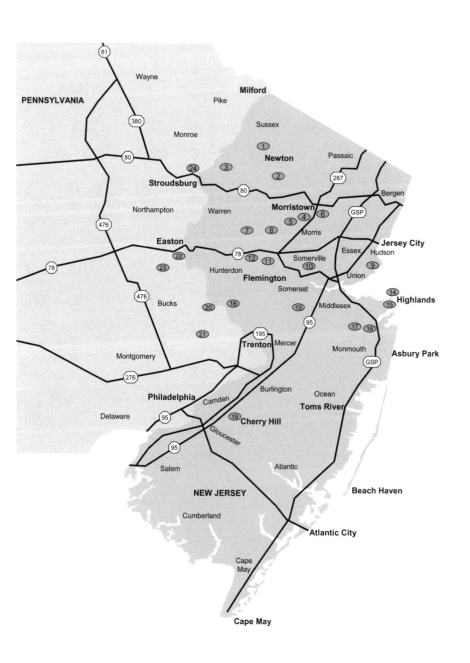

New Jersey Trails

Bridge on the Sussex Branch Trail.

1

Sussex Branch Trail

COUNTY: Sussex

TOWNS: Lockwood, Cranberry Lake, Lafayette, Branchville

TRAIL DISTANCES
Total Length 21 miles
Stanhope to Waterloo Road 2 miles
Waterloo Road to Cranberry Lake 2.2 miles
Cranberry Lake to Andover 2 miles
Andover to Newton 5.5 miles
Newton to Lafayette 4.3 miles
Lafayette to Branchville 5 miles

The Sussex Branch Trail, a rail-trail built on the old Sussex Railroad line, stretches 21 miles from Stanhope to Branchville. The history of this railroad began with another transportation system, the Morris Canal. By the 1830s, the Morris Canal connected Jersey City to the Delaware River in Phillipsburg. The canal climbed 914 feet from Jersey City to Lake Hopatcong, its primary water source, and then dropped 760 feet from the lake to the Delaware River. One of the small ports on the western half of the canal was the little town of Waterloo. And it was into Waterloo that Adam Hewitt decided to move his iron ore.

Hewitt's mine was 7 miles north in Andover and in 1848 he began construction of a mule-drawn railway to haul ore from Andover to

21

Waterloo. This small railway was chartered as the Sussex Mine Railroad. Construction of the forty-inch narrow-gauge railway was completed in 1851. It was a mule tramway for small ore cars or "jimmies." Each car had a capacity of six to eight tons and was pulled by three or four mules. Two or three hundred tons were hauled daily with a round trip requiring about five hours.

Just two years later, the railroad was renamed the Sussex Railroad and its conversion to steam locomotion began. Its charter was also expanded to include service to Newton. The Morris & Essex (M&E) line, which was also extending service to Newton, offered the Sussex a 33 percent drawback on all traffic to Waterloo if the Sussex line was open when the M&E reached Newton. Legend says that the M&E then began to pay contractors working on the Sussex line to cause delays so the M&E could reach Newton first! Hewitt suspended work at the mine and put four hundred miners to work on his railroad. The work was completed on time and the first Sussex locomotive entered Newton on November 27, 1854. The M&E opened in January 1855.

Hewitt's little railroad continued to grow and evolve despite the changing fortunes of the industries it served. Mergers, automobile use, and declining industries in Sussex County reduced service on the line through the early 1900s, but the line was not fully abandoned until 1966 by the Delaware, Lackawanna & Western (DL&W), which had gained control of the Sussex Railroad. Unfortunately, the old rail line is no longer continuous, but what is left is a designated multi-use trail maintained by Kittatinny Valley State Park. With much of its length through wildlife management areas, there are very few road crossings and it is seldom crowded, even on weekends. Porta-potties can usually be found in the parking areas. For current trail conditions, call 973-786-6445 or go to the New Jersey Parks Division website, www.state.nj.us/dep/parksandforests/.

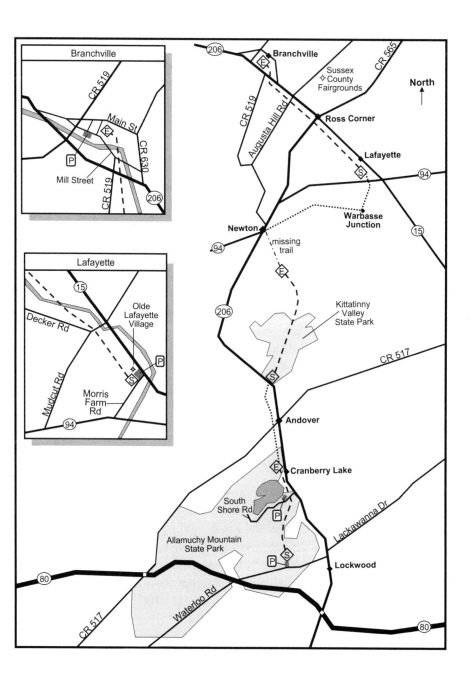

Branchville

CR 519
Main St
CR 630
P
Mill Street
CR 519
206

Lafayette

15
Olde Lafayette Village
Decker Rd
Mudcut Rd
P
Morris Farm Rd
94
S

206
Branchville
E
Sussex County Fairgrounds
CR 565
North
CR 519
Ross Corner
Augusta Hill Rd
Lafayette
94
S
Warbasse Junction
Newton
94
15
missing trail
E
Kittatinny Valley State Park
206
CR 517
S
Andover
E
Cranberry Lake
South Shore Rd
P
Lackawanna Dr
Allamuchy Mountain State Park
P
S
Lockwood
80
CR 517
Waterloo Rd
80

WATERLOO ROAD TO CRANBERRY LAKE RIDE

COUNTY: Sussex
TOWNS: Lockwood, Cranberry Lake
TYPE: out-and-back
RIDE DISTANCE: 4.4 miles
SURFACE: packed cinder
USAGE: Young Biker, Junior Biker, Preschooler, Toddler

RIDE SUMMARY

From Waterloo Road in Lockwood to Cranberry Lake and back is a short, easy ride. In most sections, the trail is packed cinder or small gravel, making it a good choice for early spring, when you are ready to blow off the winter dust. The woods along this trail are a great place to watch for deer, turkey, ducks, wild swans, foxes, raccoon, and cranes. Located at the southern end of Sussex County, this is also the most popular section of the trail, used by mountain bikers, hikers, and dog walkers. There are no road crossings except South Shore Road, and both parking lots have porta-potties. This out-and-back ride is just over 4 miles.

RIDE DETAIL

The Sussex Branch Trail is easy to find off Waterloo Road, just north of Lockwood. There is a section of trail south of Waterloo Road (on the east side of Continental Road) heading toward Stanhope but it is not maintained. There are also bike trails parallel to Waterloo Road, along the remnants of the Morris Canal. These are not part of the Sussex Branch Trail and are also not maintained.

From Waterloo Road to Cranberry Lake, the trail runs through or borders Allamuchy Mountain State Park. The surrounding area is all wetlands and small streams. All this water means insects even in early spring, so bring bug spray! At Cranberry Lake, the trail enters tiny Cranberry Lake State Park, which seems to be simply a public boat launch. Ride through the parking lot and onto the packed gravel trail around the edge of the lake. You end up in the commuter parking lot on Route 206. At this point, you should turn around. The Sussex Trail continues north of Cranberry Lake to Andover but the trail is in bad condition. It alternates between a dirt single track, with arm and leg scratching bushes, to a large ballast surface that is impossible to ride on. We also encountered several long, really muddy puddles just north of Cranberry Lake. More like lakes than puddles, these could not be avoided. Further on, the trail runs right next to Route 206. While not a safety issue, the truck and car noise was unpleasant. Closer to Andover there are several major road crossings and even worse trail conditions.

WHERE TO START

From I-80, take Exit 25 and follow Route 206 north. Just north of Lockwood, make a left on Waterloo Road (CR 604) and look for the gravel parking lot on the right.

ALTERNATE PARKING

If you want to reverse this ride, take Exit 25 from I-80 and follow Route 206 north. Just south of Cranberry Lake, make a left onto South Shore Road. The boat launch parking lot is on the right, a half mile from Route 206, with space for twenty cars and a couple of boat trailers.

KITTATINNY VALLEY STATE PARK RIDE

The middle section of the Sussex Branch Trail runs through the Kittatinny Valley State Park on its way from Andover to Newton. We often combine the rides for extra miles, starting from the state park. For details, refer to chapter 2, Kittatinny Valley State Park.

LAFAYETTE TO BRANCHVILLE RIDE

COUNTY: Sussex
TOWNS: Lafayette, Branchville
TYPE: out-and-back
RIDE DISTANCE: 10 miles
SURFACE: packed cinder, gravel
USAGE: Young Biker, Preschooler

RIDE SUMMARY

The ride from Lafayette to Branchville is a little less wooded and a little closer to the main roads. There are also more road crossings, including Route 206. The trail, with different surfaces every mile or so, meanders back and forth over the Paulinskill Creek before ending in Branchville. All the bridges were in excellent shape. Except for woods and wildlife there is very little to see, but the road crossings keep most of the equestrians and dog walkers off this section. Although it sounds boring, this 10-mile out-and-back trip makes a very nice ride and both towns are good places to visit.

A quick caution: The New Jersey State Fair is held at the Sussex County Fairgrounds during the first full week of August. With the fair and horse show, traffic in the Newton area becomes absolutely horrendous!

RIDE DETAIL

Most maps show the Sussex Trail continuing from around Townsend and Trinity Streets in Newton. Unfortunately, the trail start is well hidden and there is no parking available in the area anyway. So skip the first 4 miles and start your ride just south of Lafayette at the intersection of Route 15 and Morris Farm Road. The trail is well marked and easy to find from the road. We park at the south end of Olde Lafayette Village, which is a small collection of specialty stores and retail outlets, and walk our bikes along the road to the trail. The first section of trail is well-maintained, packed cinder that runs parallel to Route 15. There is a small road crossing after about a mile, at the town of Lafayette. If you go one block north on Mudcut Road, there are several small stores and an ice cream shop. Actually, the ice cream shop makes this one of Kevin's favorite rides, since he gets pizza in Branchville and ice cream on the way home!

Trail entrance near Lafayette.

After another mile or so, you cross Route 206 for the first time. This is a fairly easy crossing—for Route 206, anyway—thanks to the stoplight at Ross Corner. The next road crossing is Augusta Hill Road, which has a gravel parking lot on the north side. There are several bridges in this area, and although the trail runs fairly close to Routes 206 and 15, traffic noise is minimal. The last 1.5 miles of trail were not in great condition. There was a large washout area and the bushes were so close to the trail that a few timely "ducks" were required! Just south of Branchville, the trail goes under Route 206 and then ends on a small side street. There is no parking where the trail ends but there is a public parking lot just north on Mill Street. The missing component is porta-potties! Public restrooms are way back in Olde Lafayette Village.

If you want to extend this trip, the ride south from Olde Lafayette Village to the north side of Newton is about 4 miles. A mile or so south, the Sussex Branch Trail intersects the Paulinskill Valley Trail in the little town of Warbasse Junction.

WHERE TO START

From I-80, take Route 15 north and continue through Sparta. After the Route 94 intersection, make a left on Morris Farm Road. The Olde Lafayette Village parking lot is on the right.

ALTERNATE PARKING

Starting from Branchville is possible, just not convenient. Take Route 206 north and follow signs for Branchville. Make a right onto CR 630 and bear left onto Mill Street. There is a public parking area on the left. From here you must ride on the shoulder of Mill Street about two blocks east before making a left onto Milk Street to find the trail, which is *not* well marked.

If you want to shorten this ride, there is a gravel parking lot at August Hill Road. Follow Route 206 north through Ross Corner. Make a left onto August Hill Road and look for the parking lot on your right. There is space here for about five cars. The ride north to Branchville or south to Olde Lafayette Village is each about 2.5 miles.

LOCKWOOD

Lockwood is in the southern tip of Sussex County, which was officially founded in 1753 with all of six hundred inhabitants scattered about. The combination of rocky hills, numerous lakes, and conflicts with the Native Americans kept Sussex County's population low into the 1800s. Even then the terrain did not lend itself to farming, and today a visit to Sussex County is still very much a trip to the "country," although Lockwood looks pretty suburban.

FOOD, FUN, AND RESTROOMS

For restaurants and fast food, head south on Route 206 toward Stanhope, where it is a very short drive on Route 46 to Budd Lake or Ledgewood. Other options include the following:

MCDONALD'S AND DAIRY QUEEN. Take Route 206 north about a mile to the ShopRite plaza.

LOCKWOOD TAVERN AND BARONE'S. The Tavern is downstairs and has a very casual, family-friendly atmosphere with an emphasis on pizza. Barone's is upstairs, with a more formal atmosphere and an extended menu. These restaurants are north of Waterloo Road on Route 206.

RIVERSIDE PARK. This township park has a great playground, picnic tables, and a short hiking trail along the river. It is at the intersection of River and Waterloo Roads.

WATERLOO VILLAGE. This park, which is privately operated, offers a restored mid-1800s village with daily demonstrations in the blacksmith shop, gristmill, and pottery barn. The port town of Waterloo supported and was supported by the Morris Canal. Several sections of the canal and its structures, including a guard lock and inclined plane, are maintained in the park as well as a canal museum. It also has a Native American village with reproduced huts, longhouses, and dugout canoes representing Lenni Lenape life in 1625. There are two restaurants, Pavilion Café and Towpath Tavern, in the park but they are open only on weekends.

To find Waterloo Village, continue west on Waterloo Road for about a mile. Admission is charged. For more information, go to www.waterloovillage.org or call 973-347-0900.

CRANBERRY LAKE

In the early days of railroads, many built amusement or excursion parks on their lines. The Lackawanna built one of these at Cranberry Lake in 1902. The railroad leased thirty acres on a peninsula, which was reached by suspension bridge. There were stairways, platforms, and arbors built along the lakeshore and in the tree groves. A dance pavilion, boats, and a miniature steam train combined to attract large crowds. By 1903 there was also a large, lakeside hotel. After a decade or so, the resort's popularity declined. A fire in 1910 destroyed the hotel and the bridge was removed soon after. By 1920 the huge train station was replaced by a simple platform. By 1943 the station was permanently closed. Although the resort is long gone, this area still has lots to offer.

FOOD, FUN, AND RESTROOMS

CRANBERRY LAKE DELI & MARKET. This deli and convenience store is at the corner of Route 206 and Tamarak Road. If you cross the commuter parking lot, the store can be reached by bike for a quick ice cream or soda.

PORKY'S. This restaurant specializes in barbecued ribs and has a very casual, family-oriented atmosphere. It is on Route 206 about a mile south.

ANDOVER INN. Full-service, casual restaurant located on the east side of Route 206 right in the middle of Andover, which is a mile or so north.

STEWART'S ROOT BEER. This is an outdoor/indoor diner on Route 206 about two miles north of Andover.

WILD WEST CITY. This is a western style theme park featuring twenty-two daily live-action shows with shootouts, bank and train robberies, and pony, stagecoach, and miniature train rides. There is a picnic area and several fast food vendors. Open daily in the summer and on weekends in May, June, September, and October. To find this theme park, from Route 206, take Lackawanna Drive northeast for a quarter mile and look for signs. Admission is charged. For more information, go to www.wildwestcity.com or call 973-347-8900.

LAFAYETTE

FOOD, FUN, AND RESTROOMS

There are shops and restaurants in three areas. The first and closest is within Olde Lafayette Village, located near the intersection of Routes 15 and 94. The majority of the stores are retail outlets, including Big Dog Sportswear, Geoffrey Beene, and Jones New York. There are also specialty stores like Rock N' Gem, Country Mugger, and the Barkery Boutique. Kids can also have fun feeding the ducks on the small pond at the center of the village. As for restaurants, the Lafayette House, a full-service restaurant serving brunch on Sundays, is quite prominent at the south end of the village. The Jellyroll is a small café with specialty foods and gift baskets, located in the center of the village, as is Oh! Heavenly Sweets, a candy and ice cream shop. The village also hosts a farmer's market on Sundays. For more information, go to www.lafayettevillageshops.com or call 973-383-8323.

A second area to explore is the little town of Lafayette, a mile or so north on Route 15. This tiny town boasts several antiques stores and restaurants.

MILLSIDE CAFÉ. This deli, which caters to bikers, serves breakfast and lunch. They also have ice cream, sundaes, and shakes. It is located on Mudcut Road, one block north of the trail and easily accessible by bike.

CHOCOLATE GOAT GIFT SHOP. This intriguing little gift shop and specialty store has sodas, sweets, water, and much more. It is also on Mudcut Road, just off the trail.

The third area to explore is a short drive east to the little town of Franklin. Go 5 miles east on Route 94. Make a right onto North Church Road. Within a mile, you will be in Franklin at Route 23. This small town has a lot to offer.

McDonald's and Burger King. For these fast food restaurants, go north a mile on Route 23.

Franklin Mineral Museum. At one time, Franklin had the world's richest zinc mines; in fact, it took over a hundred years to deplete the mines. Thirty other unique minerals were also mined here until 1954. The mineral museum has a replica mine, a natural history collection of fossils, Native American relics, and a variety of minerals, gemstones, and crystals. It also houses fluorescent ores and minerals that emit a range of fantastic colors under ultra-violet light. Next door to the museum is the Buckwheat Dump. It contains mine tailings that can be searched for mineral specimens. Both are open from April to November, with separate admission charges. For more information, go to www.franklinmineralmuseum.com or call 973-827-3481.

BRANCHVILLE

FOOD, FUN, AND RESTROOMS

The little town of Branchville, while short of quaint, does have both full-service and fast food restaurants, and all can be reached by bike. If you want more options, take Route 206 back into Newton.

AG Pizza. Full-service, casual restaurant located between Mill and Main Streets in Branchville. There are entrances on both streets. Look for the yellow building.

Village Market. This deli and specialty market has soda, water, snacks, etc. It is also located between Mill and Main Streets with entrances on both.

Bedell's Wine & Cheese Shop. This little shop also has a deli and sells soda, juice, old-fashioned ice cream bars, snacks, and much more. It is on Main Street, just north of the square.

UPPER SPORTS DECK. This was a bit more sports bar than restaurant, but the burgers were good and the air conditioning felt great. It is just off Mill Street—go over the bridge to the gravel parking area on the left.

MCDONALD'S, BURGER KING, BASKIN-ROBBINS, DUNKIN' DONUTS. Your basic fast food selections are all available in Newton. Drive south on Route 206.

DAIRY QUEEN. The DQ is on the north side of Newton, right on Route 206. It is closer to the Route 94 intersection than the other fast food restaurants.

SPACE FARMS ZOO & MUSEUM. This zoo is owned and operated by the Space family. It is home to a variety of large cats, bear, buffalo, wolves, coyotes, yaks, and many more, while the museum, in eleven different buildings, houses memorabilia from America's past, including carriages, wagons, antique cars, weapons, and tools. The complex is open from May to October. To find the zoo from Branchville, go north on CR 519 and follow the signs. Admission is charged. For more information, visit www.spacefarms.com or call 973-875-5800.

Boat launch at Lake Aeroflex.

2

Kittatinny Valley State Park

COUNTY: Sussex

TOWN: Andover

TYPE: loop

RIDE DISTANCE: 3.5 miles

SURFACE: dirt and gravel road

USAGE: Young Biker, Preschooler

RIDE SUMMARY

The trails in Kittatinny Valley State Park offer a little of everything from rail-trail to novice mountain biking. Most of the park trails are dirt roads used by the park rangers, although some sections have a crushed gravel surface. The steeper areas can be avoided, but if you are ready for a little challenge, this is a good spot. The hilly section is bumpy but as safe as downhill gravel can get. Porta-potties are available at the Route 206 and Goodale Road parking lots. Restrooms are located near the park headquarters at the base of Lake Aeroflex.

RIDE DETAIL

Kittatinny Valley is the newest state park in New Jersey. It was acquired in 1994 through Green Acres bond funds. The main portion of the park, approximately 900 acres, was the estate of Fred Husey III, a millionaire who founded the Aeroflex Corporation. The

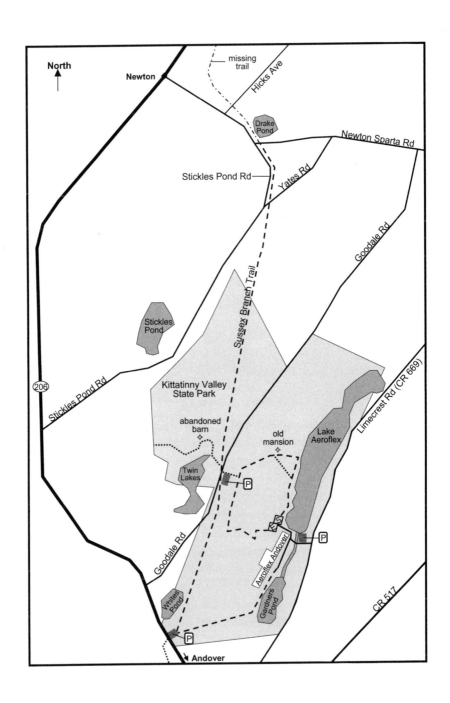

park headquarters building was his fishing clubhouse. The Aeroflex-Andover Airport is now operated by the New Jersey Forest Fire Service as a public airport and as a base for aerial forest fire fighting. This is a small airport so air traffic noise is minimal. Our kids thoroughly enjoyed watching the little planes come and go.

There are picnic areas near the park headquarters and fishing spots are easy to find along Lake Aeroflex, Twin Lakes, and Gardner's Pond. All have largemouth bass, smallmouth bass, pickerel, lake trout, brown trout, and several types of panfish. Lake Aeroflex is over a mile long and is the deepest natural lake in New Jersey, with depths of more than 100 feet. At the southern end of the lake, along the creek, there are wetland areas with a variety of frogs, turtles, snakes, and whatever else swims, hops, or slithers. Hunting for larger critters is permitted in the park *east* of Limecrest Road and *west* of Goodale Road. Neither of these areas is near the bike trails but when biking during hunting seasons extra caution is necessary. This park also contains a section of the Sussex Branch Trail so there are multiple ride possibilities. For current trail conditions, call 973-786-6445 or go to the New Jersey Parks Division website, www.state.nj.us/dep/parksandforests/.

PARK LOOP–SUSSEX BRANCH TRAIL. For a pleasant ride, minus the challenges, start at the park headquarters near the airport and go south past the end of the runway, then along the west side of Gardner's Pond. Take the second right (look for small sign). This section is all wooded with a small incline. It was a bit rocky and rutted just before the trail end at Route 206. Go across the gravel parking area and pick up the Sussex Branch Trail. Take the Sussex Trail north about a mile to Goodale Road where it intersects the Kittatinny Trail again. For a flat ride, stay on the north side of the field (parallel to the old driveway). This takes you back to the park headquarters with a total distance of around 3.5 miles. If you want a bit more, ride north on the Sussex Trail to Newton–Sparta Road, just south of Drakes Pond. This out-and-back extension adds another 4 miles.

PARK LOOP. If your young biker is ready for some rougher terrain, do the 1.5-mile loop inside the park. The trail is flat heading north along Lake Aeroflex and then across the park to Goodale Road. On the return, it is hilly and the surface is rougher. The entire trail is a road that is 8 feet across so there is plenty of room to maneuver safely. For a longer ride inside the park, cross Goodale Road and the Sussex Branch Trail and follow the gravel road through several fields, past an abandoned barn, and into the woods. This out-and-back extension adds a mile, making the entire trip about 2.5 miles.

SUSSEX BRANCH TRAIL. If you ride the Sussex Trail from the Route 206 parking lot north to Drakes Pond, it is 6 miles there and back. There are numerous mountain biking trails threading through the area so do not be disturbed by the number of mountain bikers at the Goodale Road parking lot! Look carefully for the remnants of the rail era in this section, including some impressive rock cuts. It is also possible to cross Route 206 and ride south into the little town of Andover. Within a half mile, the path gets close enough to Route 206 for you to see the businesses and restaurants in town. There are several antique and craft stores as well as restaurants there.

WHERE TO START

From Route 206, take Limecrest Road (CR 669) about 2 miles north. The parking lot is on the left. Look for signs.

ALTERNATE PARKING

There is also a Sussex Branch Trail parking lot on Route 206, just north of Andover. It is on your right, about a half mile past Limecrest Road. It is big enough to get you away from the road for unloading.

ANDOVER

FOOD, FUN, AND RESTROOMS

There are both full-service restaurants and fast food in Andover. If you ride the Sussex Branch Trail south from the Route 206 parking lot, there are several restaurants and shops accessible by bike.

ANDOVER INN. Full-service, casual restaurant located on the east side of Route 206 right in the middle of town.

ANDOVER DINER. This diner is clearly visible from the trail. It is on Route 206 just north of the main part of the town.

SONNY'S PIZZA. This is the most difficult spot to reach since it is across Route 206 in the grocery store parking lot. There is no indoor seating.

STEWART'S ROOT BEER. This is an outdoor/indoor diner on Route 206 about 2 miles north of the Sussex Branch Trail parking lot.

U-PICK STRAWBERRY FARM. The farm is open from June through August. This is a great place to pick fresh strawberries! It is on Route 206 about 2 miles north of Andover.

Trailhead sign.

3

Paulinskill Valley Trail

COUNTIES: Warren, Sussex

TOWNS: Stillwater, Blairstown, Newton

TRAIL DISTANCES
   Total Length 25 miles
   Warbasse Junction to Halsey 2.5 miles
   Halsey to Stillwater 8 miles
   Stillwater to Blairstown 6.5 miles
   Blairstown to Columbia 8 miles

Like many of the longer trails, the Paulinskill Valley Trail is an old railroad line. Its story began in 1876 when John Blair built a small steam railroad from Blairstown to the Delaware River in Columbia. In 1882 when a bridge was constructed over the river, tracks were added north of Blairstown to haul anthracite coal from Pennsylvania. The line remained active till the early 1960s. In 1992 the railroad lands, purchased using New Jersey Green Acres funds, were absorbed into the state park system. Paulinskill Valley is a designated multi-use trail, frequented by local horse owners and also popular with dog walkers, particularly around Marksboro, Blairstown, and Newton. The trail runs down the valley parallel to the Paulinskill Creek for much of the trip, and maintenance to repair wet areas seems pretty constant. This also means loose gravel that is harder to ride on but at least you stay clean! The trail crosses only a few roads, backyards, and driveways. It does not have any facilities. There are no bathrooms, no picnic areas, and no porta-potties, except in Foot Bridge Park in Blairstown and then only during the summer. The Paulinskill Valley Trail is under the jurisdiction of the Kittatinny Valley State Park. For current trail conditions, call 973-786-6445 or go to the New Jersey Parks Division website, www.state.nj.us/dep/parksandforests/.

STILLWATER TO BLAIRSTOWN RIDE

COUNTY: Warren
TOWNS: Stillwater, Blairstown
TYPE: out-and-back
RIDE DISTANCE: 13 miles
SURFACE: packed cinder
USAGE: Young Biker, Preschooler

RIDE SUMMARY

From Stillwater to Blairstown is a wonderful ride through the woods along the Paulinskill Creek, with several bridge crossings and lots of river access. Just north of Blairstown, the river is dammed, creating a long, narrow lake that is popular with fishermen and waterfowl. Riding from the middle (more or less) of the Paulinskill Trail south allows you to use Blairstown as a turn-around at 6.5 miles, or you can continue to Columbia, which is a long 14 miles south. With a packed cinder or gravel surface, the trail rides quickly; even the 13-mile trip to Blairstown and back seems fast. Blairstown has several restaurants within biking distance of the trail and there is usually a porta-potty in Foot Bridge Park.

RIDE DETAIL

Although this ride works well from either direction, we have always traveled from Stillwater south to Blairstown. There is never a problem parking at Dixon Road, across from the Water Wheel Farm

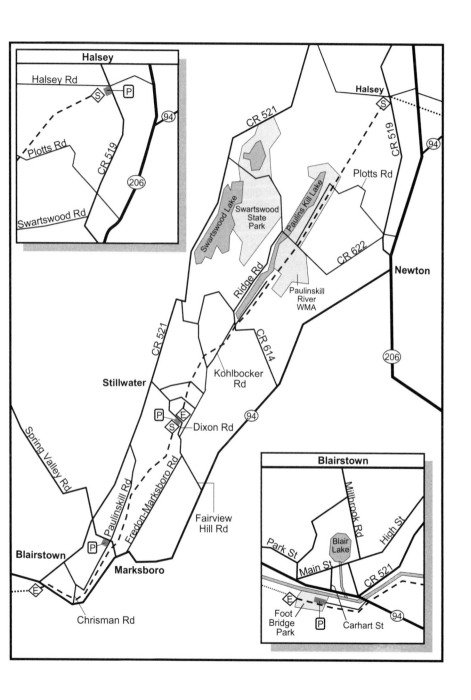

Halsey

Halsey Rd

Ⓢ Ⓟ

94

Plotts Rd

CR 519

206

Swartswood Rd

CR 521

Halsey

Ⓢ

CR 519

94

Plotts Rd

CR 622

Newton

Swartswood Lake

Swartswood State Park

Paulins Kill Lake

Ridge Rd

Paulinskill River WMA

CR 614

206

Stillwater

Kohlbocker Rd

Ⓟ Ⓔ
Ⓢ —Dixon Rd

94

CR 521

Spring Valley Rd

Paulinskill Rd

Fredon-Marksboro Rd

Fairview Hill Rd

Ⓟ

Blairstown

Ⓔ

Marksboro

Chrisman Rd

Blairstown

Millbrook Rd

High St

Park St

Blair Lake

Main St

CR 521

Ⓔ

Foot Bridge Park

Ⓟ

Carhart St

94

stable, and then Blairstown is in the middle of the ride for food, rest, and relaxation.

From the parking lot on Dixon Road, the first road crossing is Henfoot. The trail passes through someone's yard here so be sure to stay on the trail. The next road is Stillwater. Neither of these has a lot of traffic but please use caution. At about the halfway point, you cross Spring Valley Road where there is a gravel parking lot. Through here, the trail is sandwiched between the river and Paulinskill Road, which is kind of uphill out of site. Within a mile of Blairstown, you cross Chrisman Road, which has heavier traffic and the trail is not visible to drivers. Use extreme caution! Finally, the trail runs under Route 94 and down Foot Bridge Road into the park. The road, trail, and parking lot are all one so stay to the edge. There are bike racks at Foot Bridge Park along with an older playground and picnic tables. There is usually a porta-potty in the parking lot. The park gets its name from the footbridge that crosses the river here, taking you into the town.

WHERE TO START

From I-80, take Exit 4 to Route 94 North. It is 8 miles to Blairstown and 15 miles to the turn-off for the trail parking. A few miles past the little town of Marksboro, make a left onto Fairview Hill Road, which is a small country road that is easily missed. Go about a mile to Fredon–Marksboro Road and make a right. Make the next left onto Dixon Road. The parking area is down the hill on the left. There is space here for ten cars at most.

ALTERNATE PARKING

If you choose to start in Blairstown, use Foot Bridge Park. From I-80, take Exit 4 to Route 94 North. Just after the intersection with CR 521, make a right turn onto Foot Bridge Road, which is also the trail, so please drive slowly. Continue straight one block (past the offices and stores) to the parking area. The trail goes both north and south here.

If you want a shorter ride, start in Marksboro, at the parking area on Spring Valley Road. From Route 94 heading north, turn left onto Spring Valley Road and continue across the river. The parking area is at the bottom of the hill, on your left. There is parking here for six cars. Blairstown is about 3 miles south, making this a nice, short 6-mile out-and-back.

HALSEY TO STILLWATER RIDE

COUNTY: Sussex
TOWNS: Newton, Stillwater
TYPE: out-and-back
RIDE DISTANCE: 16 miles
SURFACE: packed cinder, dirt single track
USAGE: Young Biker, Preschooler

RIDE SUMMARY

From Halsey (just north of Newton) south to Stillwater is another lovely ride through the woods and then through even more woods! These 8 miles make a nice change from all the flat, open canal trails and can be absolutely wonderful in early spring or in the fall when the trees change color. There are several small upgrades (certainly not hills but *up* nonetheless) and a bit more of a grade than on most rail-trails. There are a number of road crossings, of which two require short bypasses to the nearest road due to missing bridges. The surface on this section varied considerably from a cut-up single track to double track to packed cinder, and there are no facilities, although Newton provides lots of choices for food and fun. And keep in mind when planning this ride, the New Jersey State Fair is held at the Sussex County Fairgrounds during the first full week of August. Most of the roads become parking lots by midday.

RIDE DETAIL

This ride can be done in either direction. If you are combining your ride with a visit to Swartswood State Park, use Stillwater as your starting point rather than Halsey, but be aware that there are no facilities, no restaurants, no *nothing* in the area. This is horse country, and even gas stations and convenience stores are few and far between. There are multiple starting points east of Route 206, but all require crossing Routes 206 and 94. For these reasons, we have always started from the parking area in Halsey, which allows us to use Newton for food and fun.

The parking lot at Halsey is large, easy to find, and big enough to allow safe unloading/loading with kids. From the parking lot, go southwest, away from Newton, and in 2 miles the trail intersects Plotts Road. The trail crosses at an angle here and cars cannot see you. Please use extra caution. In the next mile or so the trail runs parallel to Spirol Road, which borders the Paulinskill River Wildlife Management Area (WMA). This is a quiet, wooded area with little traffic or noise. The next road is CR 622 (Newton–Swartswood Road) and, as its name implies, it is a cut-through road with heavy traffic. It is a nice long run to the next road crossing at CR 614 (Paulinskill Road) but the bridge is missing here. As you pass the end of the lake, drop down onto South Shore Terrace, cross CR 614, and then rejoin the trail from Kohlbocker Road. There are very obvious short-cuts to the road and back up to the trail but the cuts are narrow and a bit steep, particularly if you are towing a cart. In the last couple of miles to the Dixon Road parking area, there are four small road crossings. Due to horse traffic and washouts, some of the worst trail conditions were within the last half mile to Water Wheel Farm, where there is a picnic table or two but no porta-potties. The roundtrip is 16 miles.

If you want to extend your ride, the Paulinskill Valley Trail continues south from Stillwater. Refer to the Stillwater to Blairstown Ride above.

WHERE TO START

Take Route 206 to Newton and continue north through town. After the Route 94 intersection, make a left on CR 626 (Halsey Road). At the next stoplight, look for the gravel parking lot on the left. The trail crosses CR 519 here so it is well marked.

STILLWATER

FOOD, FUN, AND RESTROOMS

This area has very limited possibilities. Once you get north of Blairstown, horse stables and dairy farms dominate the landscape until you reach Newton.

MARKSBORO DELI. There is a small deli on Route 94 in Marksboro, right before the turn onto Spring Valley Road.

WATER WHEEL FARM. This is the large farm that encompasses most of the land from Fredon–Marksboro Road to Dixon Road. It is easy to spot as all the farm buildings are painted red. The barn closest to the parking area is a boarding stable but it is not open to the public. There is also a small petting zoo with rabbits, llamas, emus, and several other baby animals at the corner of Dixon and Pruder Roads. Look for the rabbit cages facing Pruder Road. Any animal can bite so remember to keep little fingers away from the fence.

BLAIRSTOWN

FOOD, FUN, AND RESTROOMS

This small town packs a lot into one block! Walk across the foot-bridge to reach Route 94 and bear right up Carhart Street. Within one block is Main Street. Take time to explore the old mill built by John Blair in 1889, Blair Lake, and a few of the shops, which include a bookstore, book café, restaurant, and several small gift stores.

FOOT BRIDGE PARK. The parking area used to be the railroad station for the Blairstown Railroad. There was a two-story passenger station and an "armstrong" turntable. These old turntables were used to turn the stream locomotives around and were operated by men with *strong arms*. As with most railroad terminals, there was also a freight house for goods shipped by rail, a creamery, and lumber and coal yards. All of these old structures were abandoned, and in the 1970s the town tore them down to clean up the area for Foot Bridge Park. This is a very good place to rest and perhaps have a picnic lunch.

BLAIRSTOWN DINER. This diner is on Route 94 and is visible from the park.

BLAIRSTOWN INN. This full-service restaurant is also visible from the park and is just a block south on Route 94.

POST TIME PUB. Though closed on Sunday, this restaurant and pub is a great choice any other day. It is on Main Street about a block south of Bridge Street.

FRANK'S PIZZA. Go 3 miles south on Route 94 to the A&P shopping center. This eat-in pizzeria is a great place to feed the kids so they sleep all the way home.

DOGHOUSE DELI & BAGEL SHOP. This eat-in deli is on Route 94 across the street from the A&P shopping center, which is 3 miles south of town.

DAIRY QUEEN. The DQ is also on Route 94 but is 5 miles south of town. Freestanding, it is easy to spot.

MCDONALD'S. The nearest fast food is just off I-80 at the intersection of Route 94 in Columbia. Follow signs for I-80 West and then towards Columbia instead of getting on I-80.

NEWTON

FOOD, FUN, AND RESTROOMS

This town offers everything from fast food to specialty restaurants. The fast food restaurants, including McDonald's, Burger King, Dunkin' Donuts, and Baskin-Robbins, are all on Route 206 just north of town. This area is also good for fun, should your bike ride be shortened or abandoned for the day.

PIZZA HUT. This restaurant is located on Route 206 across from the Weiss Market.

DAIRY QUEEN. The DQ is just a bit further north of the other restaurants, but is still south of the Route 94 intersection. Freestanding, it is hard to miss.

CHATTERBOX DINER. This is an old-fashioned fifties-style diner complete with outside car service with waitresses on roller skates, big booths, and a jukebox. The menu is true to the period and the atmosphere is pure fun. It is located where Routes 206 and 15 intersect, about 3 miles north of Newton.

NEW JERSEY CARDINALS. This minor league team is affiliated with the St. Louis Cardinals and is part of the New York–Penn League. They play from mid-June to early September. Many of the games are in the late afternoon or early evening, and tickets are still reasonable. For more information, go to www.njcards.com or call 973-579-7500.

SUSSEX COUNTY FAIRGROUNDS. This county fairground has a full calendar of events, including craft, dog, and horse shows, concerts, demolition derbies, and even a crawdad festival. It is also the site of the New Jersey State Fair in early August. From Route 206, go north on Augusta Hill Road. For more information, visit www.sussex-county-fair.org or call 973-948-5500.

SWARTSWOOD STATE PARK. Well known for fishing, swimming, and quiet trail walks, this park encompasses two lakes: Swartswood and Little Swartswood. It was established in 1914 as New Jersey's first state park and is open year-round. There is a lifeguard at the swimming beach, open only in the summer. There are picnic areas throughout the park and grills are available at every site. For the main entrance, follow CR 519 for approximately half a mile, then make a left onto CR 622 at the Sussex County College sign. Follow CR 622 for about 4 miles. Turn left onto CR 619. The park entrance is about half a mile south on Route 619. An admission fee is charged from Memorial to Labor Day.

Playground at South Street Park.

4

Loantaka Brook Reservation

COUNTY: Morris

TOWN: Morristown

TYPE: out-and-back

RIDE DISTANCE: 8 miles

SURFACE: pavement

USAGE: Young Biker, Junior Biker, Preschooler, Toddler

RIDE SUMMARY

Loantaka Brook Reservation is actually three parks, which combine for some very nice biking for all types of bikers at all times of the year. The paved path crosses several streams as it meanders through the woods and fields of these parks. There are restrooms at South Street Park and Loantaka Brook Park. Porta-potties are scattered here and there. It is, of course, also very popular but seems to absorb bikers and hikers without feeling crowded.

RIDE DETAIL

Loantaka Brook Reservation is part of the Morris County Park system. Located along Loantaka Brook, the 570-acre preserve consists of four areas: Seaton Hackney Riding Stables, the South Street Recreation Area, Loantaka Brook Park, and the Loantaka Way trail access area, which extends south to Green Village Road. At South

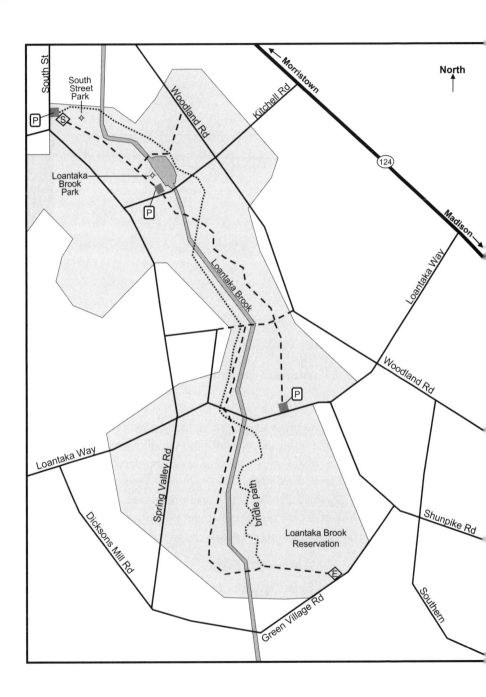

North

Morristown

Madison

124

South St

South Street Park

Woodland Rd

Kitchell Rd

Loantaka Way

Loantaka Brook Park

Loantaka Brook

Woodland Rd

Loantaka Way

Spring Valley Rd

Dicksons Mill Rd

bridle path

Loantaka Brook Reservation

Shunpike Rd

Southern

Green Village Rd

Street Park, there is a very nice playground area, ball fields, picnic area, and restrooms. Loantaka Brook Park, located on Kitchell Road, has ball fields, picnic areas, a small lake, and restrooms at the north end. There are no facilities at the parking lot on Loantaka Way and no parking at Green Village Road.

Starting at South Street Park, follow the paved path south to Loantaka Brook Park and continue past the pond and across the parking area. Once you cross Kitchell Road, the trail goes south for about a mile to the main "intersection," where two paved paths cross. Make a right (west), cross the creek, and continue south on the trail to Loantaka Way, which must be crossed on your way south to Green Village Road. It is about 8 miles roundtrip. If you miss the turn or just want to extend your ride a bit, go straight at the main intersection in the park. You end up in the parking area at Loantaka Way, which adds a mile or so. For current trail information, check with the Morris County Park Commission at www.parks.morris.nj.us or call 973-326-7600.

BRIDLE PATH LOOP. You can create a loop by riding south on the paved path and north on the bridle path, which is a dirt "mountain biking" path with roots, puddles, and a stream crossing. It is flat and provides a nice challenge for young bikers or adventurous preschoolers! Kathleen loved this ride and demanded repeats of the stream crossing. The bridle path begins about a half mile north of Green Village Road. The path returns north, crossing Loantaka Way at the same point as the paved trail, and goes around the east side of the lake to where it ends behind the restrooms at South Street Park. This is about 9 miles roundtrip.

WHERE TO START

From I-287 South, take Exit 35 to Route 124 (Madison Avenue). At the light, go west one block and make a left onto South Street. From I-287 North, take Exit 35 to South Street and continue south. The parking lot, which has space for forty or more cars, is on South Street on the left, just past Seaton Hackney Stables.

ALTERNATE PARKING

If you want to use Loantaka Brook Park as your starting point, go east on Route 124 toward Madison. Make a right onto Kitchell Road. The parking lot, which is quite large, is on your right.

If you want to start in the middle, use the parking area on Loantaka Way. From Route 124, take Loantaka Way west to the small parking area, with space for only twenty cars.

MORRISTOWN

FOOD, FUN, AND RESTROOMS

Like most county parks, Loantaka Brook is buffered from commercial districts. Morristown, however, has numerous restaurants, from delis and ice cream shops to five-star restaurants. I selected these simply because they have easy parking. South Street merges into Route 124 just west of I-287.

PALMER'S COUNTRY DELI. This deli has subs, bagels, snacks, and drinks. It is located on South Street, about a half mile north of the park.

CALALOO CAFÉ. This full-service restaurant in Morristown is on South Street about a mile from South Street Park. It has a fun, casual atmosphere.

BASKIN-ROBBINS. Located in Morristown, it is on South Street about 2 miles from the park. Look for parking on the side street.

MORRISTOWN DELI. This deli is more like a restaurant with an expanded menu and inside seating. It is at the intersection of South and Elm Streets.

BURGER KING. The closest BK is located near the Morristown train station in a small strip mall. Follow South Street into Morristown—about 2 miles—and then make a right onto Elm Street. At the next light, make a left onto Morris Street (CR 510).

THE OFFICE. This is a full-service restaurant on the village green. Use the public parking area one block southwest near the corner of Market and Maple Streets.

BENNIGAN'S. This restaurant is located in Headquarters Plaza, which is north of the village green, on Route 202. If you park in the HQ Plaza, there are several other restaurants across the street from which to choose.

5

Patriots' Path–Morristown

COUNTY: Morris

TOWN: Morristown

TYPE: out-and-back

RIDE DISTANCE: 5.5 miles

SURFACE: pavement, crushed stone

USAGE: Young Biker, Preschooler

RIDE SUMMARY

Patriots' Path is a network of trails connecting many of the parks and historic sites in Morris County. Unfortunately, few sections are suitable for family biking. The exception begins across the street from Historic Speedwell and runs 2.5 miles or so west through the residential area north of Morristown. While the surface is paved, it is not always smooth. In fact the tree roots growing under the pavement made some wooded areas so bumpy it was tempting to walk. On the plus side, multiple little bridges provide access to the Whippany River and all the street crossings are small, local roads. You may encounter numerous joggers and dog walkers but you will not find restrooms, porta-potties, or restaurants within biking distance of the trail. Fortunately, Morristown has a lot to offer to round out the day.

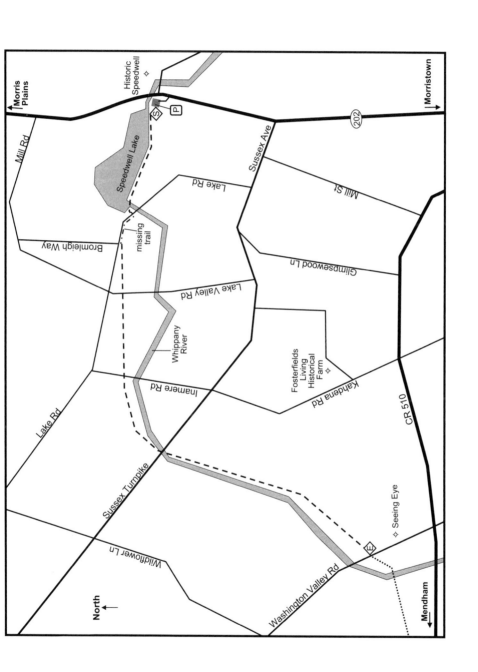

Morris Plains

Morristown

Mill Rd

Historic Speedwell ◇

Speedwell Lake

S

P

Sussex Ave

202

Lake Rd

Mill St

Bromleigh Way

missing trail

Glimpsewood Ln

Lake Valley Rd

Whippany River

Inamere Rd

Fosterfields Living Historical Farm ◇

Kahdena Rd

Lake Rd

CR 510

Sussex Turnpike

Seeing Eye ◇

Wildflower Ln

E

Washington Valley Rd

Mendham

North

RIDE DETAIL

Patriots' Path, which begins at Speedwell Lake in Morristown, is an evolving network of trails being assembled by the Morris County Park Commission. It will eventually link dozens of parks and other points of interest in Morris County. Today, there are about 20 miles of continuous (I use this term loosely here!) trails from Morristown to Chester. Unfortunately, many sections are best suited to mountain bikes or horses while sections with better surfaces are short or not well marked.

From Speedwell Lake to Washington Valley Road, the trail is mostly paved and easy to travel. The Patriots' Path map shows this section as continuous. It is not! There is a short section missing along Lake Road. There is one upgrade south of Sussex Turnpike but it is not steep, just uphill a bit. Most of this section is flat since it is built on the old right-of-way for the Rockaway Valley Railroad. This little railroad, nicknamed the "Rockabye Baby," struggled into existence in the late 1800s and survived for about thirty years, primarily as an agricultural railroad running from Whitehouse to Morristown. Near Speedwell Lake, the path is easily recognized as a rail-trail. For current trail conditions, check with the Morris County Park Commission at www.parks.morris.nj.us or call 973-326-7600.

WHERE TO START

From I-80, take Exit 42 and follow Route 202 south toward Morristown. At Speedwell Lake, immediately across the street from Historic Speedwell, there is a large gravel parking lot.

MORRISTOWN

Morristown is one of the most historically significant sites in the nation. The town played a prominent role in the Revolutionary War, housed more millionaires than any other city in the Gilded Age, and spawned the telegraph, the steamship engine, and the modern version of Santa Claus. Almost every street in Morristown, including the 285-year-old village green, has some historic character or significance, and many of these sites are (or soon will be) linked by Patriots' Path. While we do not recommend trying to reach them by bike, there are many historical sites worth visiting.

FOOD, FUN, AND RESTROOMS

Morristown has numerous restaurants from deli's and ice cream shops to five-star restaurants. I have listed several below that have easy parking. In downtown Morristown, use the parking garage in Headquarters Plaza or the public parking lot one block southwest of the village green, which is a mile south of Historic Speedwell on Route 202. Morris Plains, which is about a mile north on Route 202, has several options from pizza to full-service restaurants. Park on the side roads where allowed.

BENNIGAN'S. This restaurant is located in Headquarters Plaza, which is north of the village green, on Route 202. If you park in the HQ Plaza, there are several other restaurants across the street from which to choose.

BURGER KING. The BK is in a strip mall near the Morristown train station. Follow Route 202 south about a mile and then go left on Spring Street (at the fork). Continue uphill, bear left at the light, and look for the strip mall on your left.

BASKIN-ROBBINS. It is on South Street about two blocks south of the village green. Look for parking on the side street.

ARTHUR'S STEAKHOUSE. This famous steakhouse is on Route 202, a mile north of Speedwell in downtown Morris Plains. It is across the street from the train station. They do *not* take credit cards.

COLLINS PUB. This is a little, casual pub on Route 202 in Morris Plains. It is across the street from the train station.

FOSTERFIELDS LIVING HISTORICAL FARM. Fosterfields offers a glimpse of life on a farm in the late nineteen century. Walking on the grounds, it is easy to imagine what it was like for Caroline Foster, who lived there for ninety-eight years. The farm is open Wednesday–Sunday from April to October and their calendar is packed with special events. Admission is charged. For more information, call 973-326-7645. It is located on Kahdena Road, just off CR 510.

THE SEEING EYE. Another excellent option is to schedule a tour of the Seeing Eye. These are available Mondays and Thursdays for children nine years and older. Please contact the Seeing Eye ahead of time, as reservations are required. For more information, go to www.seeingeye.org or call 973-539-4425.

SPEEDWELL IRON WORKS. The Speedwell National Historic Site preserves part of the estate of Stephen Vail, owner of the Speedwell Iron Works. In 1815 Vail became the sole owner of the iron works, and the forge soon prospered. By 1829 he also owned the property on the eastern side of the road, which included a cotton mill. In time, the farm, mill, and forge became known as Judge Vail's Homestead Farm, which quickly became a major industrial center, responsible for several major advances in technology.

SS *Savannah.* In 1818 Stephen Vail was contracted by the Savannah Steam Ship Company to assemble a steam engine for the SS *Savannah,* the first steamship built for Atlantic crossings. On May 22, 1819, the *Savannah* put to sea with "steam and sails" on her historic voyage and arrived at Liverpool, England, in 29 days and 4 hours. The steam engine was used on 18 days of the trip. Steam power was so unusual that when the *Savannah* was sighted off the coast of England, a signal station attendant assumed the ship was on fire. A cutter was dispatched to rescue the ship! Though the crossing was a success, Americans were not ready to trust steam power, and the steam engine was removed before the *Savannah's* next voyage.

Telegraph. History credits Samuel Morse with the invention of the telegraph, but he would not have succeeded without Stephan Vail and his son, Alfred. In 1837 they entered into an agreement with Morse to begin construction. Over the next several years, Alfred Vail, Morse, and others conquered numerous technical challenges to develop the first commercially viable telegraph. On January 6, 1838, Stephan Vail sent the first message, "A patient waiter is no loser." Several days later the public crowded the second floor of the factory to witness Morse and Vail sending and receiving messages through two miles of wire strung in circles around the room. Five years after the first demonstration, Congress passed a bill providing funds to construct a telegraph line from Washington, D.C., to Baltimore. This line became operational on May 24, 1844. For another five years, Vail continued improving the telegraph and line designs. Today, the factory is a National Historic Landmark and the telegraph exhibits are located in the same room where Vail and Morse worked.

Visitors to Historic Speedwell can also explore the iron works, carriage house, granary, and an exhibit on the SS *Savannah*. There is a gift shop and guided tours through the Vail Mansion are available. There is usually a porta-potty in the parking area. For more information, go to www.speedwell.org or call 973-540-0211.

Alfred Vail's laboratory.

6

Traction Line Trail

COUNTY: Morris

TOWN: Morristown

TYPE: out-and-back

RIDE DISTANCE: 5 miles

SURFACE: pavement

USAGE: Young Biker, Junior Biker, Preschooler, Toddler

RIDE SUMMARY

This recreation trail runs parallel to the New Jersey Transit tracks from Morristown to the north edge of Madison. The paved path is flat and there is an 8-foot-high, chain-link fence on both sides, keeping people and creatures away from the tracks. The paved surface is in excellent condition, making it a good choice for junior bikers and toddlers. It is not particularly scenic but my kids enjoyed seeing the station and trains up close (very up close). Usage is light to moderate, mostly by joggers who live in the area. There are no restrooms or porta-potties.

RIDE DETAIL

Strangely enough, this particular trail is not a rail-trail. It is a Morris County Park recreation trail constructed on the empty, unused land

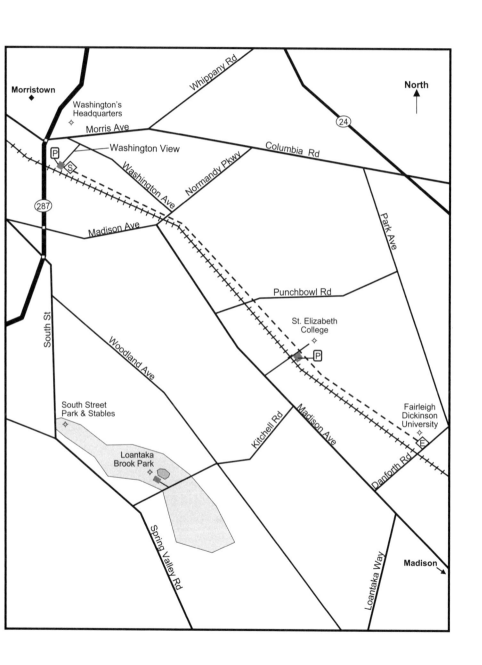

along the New Jersey Transit railroad line. The trail begins on the east side of I-287. The parking lot, which has about ten spots, actually backs up to the highway, although it is very well hidden inside an apartment complex. The trail, however, is easy to spot from the parking area and runs next to the New Jersey Transit tracks for 2.5 miles. In some places there are grassy areas between the trail and tracks. In others, the trail is very close to the tracks. The fence ensures that kids are safe, and there are underpasses at Normandy Parkway and Punchbowl Road. You do have to cross the entrance/exit for the College of St. Elizabeth. Due to the columns, drivers on the entrance road cannot see the trail so use extra caution. The trail ends just north of Madison, at Danforth Road. There is no parking at the southern end.

We did wait until midday to do the ride. This is a commuter line and we wanted to avoid the early morning trains, although the schedule is lighter on weekends. The kids, of course, thought racing a train a fabulous idea! We also noted that a large majority of the trail is in the open with very little shade. For current trail conditions, check with Morris County Park Commission at www.parks.morris.nj.us or call 973-326-7600.

While both Morristown and Madison offer any number of attractions and eating options, none are within biking distance of the trail. Furthermore, the fence, while keeping you safe, prevents access to any of the restaurants along Madison Avenue (Route 124).

Where to Start

From I-287, take Exit 36A to Morris Avenue. Make the first right onto Washington Avenue. Look for the statue of George Washington. Then make an immediate right onto Washington View. The parking lot is at the end of this road.

Alternate Parking

The only other option for parking (in the unlikely event the north lot is full) is the New Jersey Transit lot near the College of St. Elizabeth.

This is a huge parking area but it is only an option on weekends or late evening during the week. It is about a mile or so south of Morristown on Madison Avenue.

MORRISTOWN

Morristown is strategically located about 50 miles from Trenton and roughly 26 miles from New York City. It was settled in the early 1700s and fifty years later had become a thriving township. The First Presbyterian Church, located on the village green, was erected in 1740, and the Courthouse was built in 1755. Thus, during the Revolutionary War, it was logical for General George Washington to select Morristown as his headquarters after the Battles of Trenton and Princeton. Washington's army camped outside Morristown for the first time in January 1777. Washington used Freeman's Tavern as his headquarters that first winter.

FOOD, FUN, AND RESTROOMS

You should definitely reserve time in the day to visit Morristown, which has historic sites on almost every street and wonderful restaurants and delis tucked in between. For the downtown area, including the village green, go west on Morris Avenue (back over I-287).

BURGER KING. The nearest BK in Morristown is near the railroad station. It is on Morris Avenue about a mile west of I-287.

FRIENDLY'S. This restaurant/ice cream shop is visible from the trail, but you cannot get there by bike without riding on Normandy Parkway. Located at the corner of Madison Avenue and Normandy Parkway, it is just minutes away by car.

GROUND ROUND. This family-oriented restaurant is on Ridgedale Avenue. Take Morris Avenue west, make a right onto Ridgedale Avenue, and go 1 mile north. The restaurant is in the mall at the intersection with Hanover Avenue.

FRELINGHUYSEN ARBORETUM. Open daily, this Morris County Park has walking trails, greenhouses, special events and displays, and a gift shop. To get to the arboretum, go east on Morris Avenue, bear left onto Whippany Avenue, and then make a left onto East Hanover. Look for the entrance across from the county library.

MORRIS MUSEUM. This local museum has permanent exhibits in the areas of natural science, rocks, minerals, dinosaurs, fossils, dolls, and toys, as well as an American Indian Gallery and a Children's Room. Check the events calendar for rotating exhibits. For more information, call 973-971-3700 or visit www.morrismuseum.org. To get to the museum, go east on Morris Avenue, bear right onto Columbia Road, and make a left onto Normandy Heights Road.

WASHINGTON'S HEADQUARTERS. During the winter of 1779, Washington used this big, white mansion, which was constructed in 1774 by Colonel Jacob Ford, as his headquarters. The Fords were a wealthy, prominent family in Morristown and their home was one of the finest in the country. Ford passed away in January of 1777, however, and General Washington rented the house from his widow. Mrs. Ford and her children crammed into two rooms during Washington's stay to provide space for the general's officers and staff. Open all year except on major holidays, the house is now part of the Morristown National Historic Park. For more information, go to www.nps.gov/morr/ or call 973-539-2016.

JOCKEY HOLLOW. This park contains replicas of the soldiers' huts used by the Continental Army during the winter encampments of 1777 and 1779, as well as the Tempe Wick farm, which housed one of Washington's officers. There are over 20 miles of hiking trails, and this national park connects to Lewis Morris Park, a county park with picnic areas, playgrounds, and more hiking trails. Restrooms are located at the visitor center. The entrance is off Tempe Wick Road. Take Route 202 west about 4 miles from Morristown. Follow the signs. Jockey Hollow is part of the Morristown National Historic Park and is open all year except on major holidays. For more information, go to www.nps.gov/morr/ or call 973-539-2016.

FORT NONSENSE. In May 1777, this small hill throbbed with activity as soldiers dug trenches and raised embankments. General Washington ordered the crest fortified as it strategically overlooked the town and allowed a view of the main road to New York City. Legend says the earthworks became known as Fort Nonsense because it was built only to keep the troops occupied. There are no facilities at this small park, which is located on Ann Street. From Morristown, take Madison Avenue (Route 124) west and make a left onto Western Avenue. Follow the signs.

7

Columbia Trail

COUNTIES: Morris, Hunterdon

TOWNS: Flanders, Long Valley, Califon, High Bridge

TRAIL DISTANCES:
Total Length 15 miles
Flanders to Long Valley 4 miles
Long Valley to Califon 6 miles
Califon to High Bridge 5 miles

The Columbia Trail was once the High Bridge Branch of the Central Railroad of New Jersey. Constructed in the 1850s, this railway was used to move ore from mines further north, although it also served the icehouses, creameries, and peach growers of Morris and Hunterdon Counties. Following the South Branch of the Raritan River, the remaining right-of-way runs from Flanders to High Bridge. Almost any section provides a quiet, scenic ride with lots of wildlife. Designated as a multi-use trail, most of it is well maintained since the Columbia Gas Company uses it to access their pipeline. The surface varies considerably along the 15 miles. There are road crossings every so often and several bridges, all in good condition. The towns have good food stops but there are no porta-potties or restrooms along the trail. Any of these rides can be combined, or alternate parking selected, to change the length of your trip, depending on the weather and how far you want to go. For current

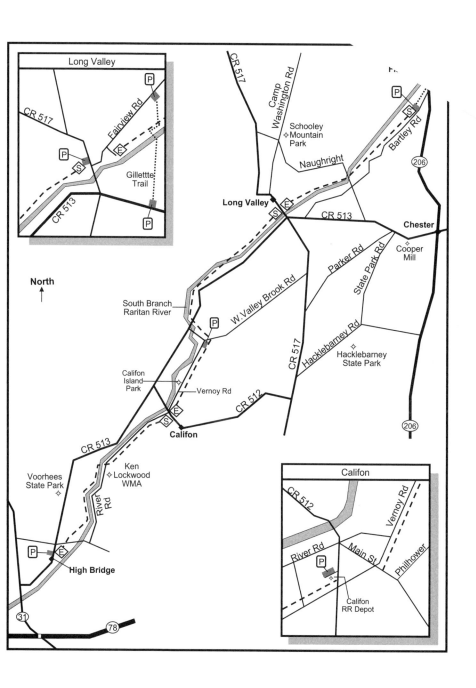

trail conditions, check the Hunterdon County park system website, www.co.hunterdon.nj.us/depts/parks/parks.htm or call 908-782-1158.

FLANDERS TO LONG VALLEY RIDE

COUNTY: Morris
TOWNS: Flanders, Long Valley
TYPE: out-and-back
RIDE DISTANCE: 8 miles
SURFACE: single track, packed gravel
USAGE: Young Biker, Preschooler

RIDE SUMMARY

From Flanders to Long Valley is a short, scenic ride. Parking at the fishing access lot is easy and the trail runs along the river. The surface is dirt single track for the first half and packed gravel for the second half. It is exceptionally wide and mostly wooded. There are two road crossings at the east end but the majority of the ride is through the woods with no road crossings. No restrooms or porta-potties are available but Long Valley provides several good food stops.

RIDE DETAIL

This trail section is part of the Morris County park system and is a designated multi-use trail. There are several large horse stables bordering the trail so horseback riders are common. Occasionally, we have encountered dog walkers in this section but mostly we see only one to two individuals for the entire ride.

There are several very good parking spots, all on or just off major roads. Where the rail line crosses Bartley Road, there is a small, unmarked gravel parking lot. The trail begins here and has a loose gravel surface. About a half mile further west is the fishing access parking area, which is not on the road and provides a much safer spot to unload kids and bikes. Starting here, the surface is packed gravel but after the first road, Four Bridges, it changes from gravel to a dirt single track. After the Naughright Road crossing, the trail surface switches from single track to packed gravel with a few really irritating loose gravel sections. About 3.5 miles into the trip, the Columbia Trail intersects the Gillette Trail coming across from the parking lot on Fairview Road. Within 100 feet or so, the Gillette Trail turns left, heading for the parking lot on CR 513. The Gillette trailheads make good starting points if you want to ride toward Flanders instead. There is usually a porta-potty at the parking area on Fairview Road.

Unfortunately, just before Long Valley, the Columbia Trail more or less disappears. There are two factories, a metal-working company, and what appears to be an abandoned dairy, which have incorporated the trail into their parking lots. You can ride across the parking lots and end up on Fairview Road but a better choice is to make a right at the first building's driveway. Ride up the driveway and follow Fairview Road to CR 517 (Schooley Mountain Road). Fairview Road does not have much in the way of traffic and a short road ride is better than a popped tire.

Getting to the restaurants in town is tough on a bike since the roads here are very busy. Park your bikes in the Columbia Trail gravel lot, opposite the county tax office on CR 517, and walk south one block to CR 513 where there are a few small shops, a gas station with a mini-mart, and several restaurants.

If you want to extend your ride from Long Valley, go north a short block along CR 517 to where the Columbia Trail continues toward Califon. Look for the gravel parking lot, opposite the county tax office.

WHERE TO START

From I-80, take Exit 27 to Route 206 and go south into Flanders. At the light just south of town, make a right onto Bartley Road. At the next intersection (less than a mile) and just after you cross the railroad tracks, make a left turn. Go another mile on Bartley River Road. The fishing access parking lot is on the right. Look for a park sign.

LONG VALLEY TO CALIFON RIDE

COUNTY: Hunterdon
TOWNS: Long Valley, Califon
TYPE: out-and-back
RIDE DISTANCE: 12 miles
SURFACE: crushed gravel or packed dirt
USAGE: Young Biker, Preschooler

RIDE SUMMARY

The Columbia Trail section running from Long Valley to Califon is very well maintained, lightly used, mostly wooded, and a wonderful little trip. Many sections parallel the South Branch of the Raritan River, although there is no real access to the river. All the bridges are in good condition. There are a few road crossings, but most are small local roads except for CR 513, which must be crossed north of Califon. This trail offers several options if you want to do a loop or extend the ride. There are no porta-potties or restrooms at the access points.

RIDE DETAIL

This stretch from Long Valley south into Califon is one of our favorite rides. There are several parking options around Long Valley, the easiest being right on CR 517. The trail goes south, crisscrossing the river and a few extended driveways before ending in downtown Califon. Where the trail intersects CR 513, it disappears for a short distance, directly across from the Robert Jenkinson Nursery. Walk parallel to the nursery on CR 513. Turn left at the kennel fence onto the grass single track and follow the kennel property line (on your right) for about 100 feet. The trail reappears (Da-dah!) on your right at the end of the fence line. A little further on, the trail merges onto Vernoy Road for a short while. Watch for the brown Columbia Trail sign, which will get you back on the trail (versus staying on the road) for the last half mile to "downtown" Califon.

VERNOY ROAD LOOP. This road is an exception to my *no roads* rule since there are no houses, minimal traffic, and you must ride a portion of it anyway just north of Califon. If you ride the road, you pass Califon Island Park, which is a town park right along the river with picnic grounds, ball fields, and a playground area that is first-rate. The park is about a half mile north of town. It is also possible to stay on Vernoy Road for 2 miles (past the first intersection with the Columbia Trail) until you reach W. Valley Brook Road. If you turn right at this intersection, the trail is easy to access again where it crosses W. Valley Brook Road. There is a small gravel parking lot here.

WHERE TO START

From I-80, take Exit 27 and follow Route 206 south. In Chester, make a right (west) onto CR 513. In Long Valley, go one block north on CR 517. There is a small gravel lot on your left, across from the county tax office.

ALTERNATE PARKING

There is a gravel parking area for the Gillette Trail on CR 513 near the intersection of CR 513 and Bartley Road. The parking lot, which has space for about eight cars, is marked with a Patriots' Path/Gillette Trail sign. From this parking lot, follow the gravel road/truck track across the field (parallel to the farm), through the old orchard, into the woods, over the bridge, and then up to the Columbia Trail. The last part can be a bit mucky and rough but it is short.

Another choice in Long Valley is to park at the Gillette Trail parking lot on Fairview Road. From Long Valley, go north on CR 517 and make a right onto Fairview Road. Follow this road out of town for a mile or so. The gravel parking area is easy to spot on your right. There is usually a porta-potty here. From this lot, follow the grass trail south to the Columbia Trail.

CALIFON TO HIGH BRIDGE RIDE

COUNTY: Hunterdon
TOWNS: Califon, High Bridge
TYPE: out-and-back
RIDE DISTANCE: 10 miles
SURFACE: crushed gravel, packed dirt
USAGE: Young Biker, Preschooler

RIDE SUMMARY

In the lower or southwest section, the trail is in good condition with a packed gravel surface. Most of the ride is through the Ken Lockwood Wildlife Management Area (WMA). There is only one road crossing in this section. More people use this end of the Columbia Trail and there are frequently hikers and dog walkers near High Bridge. There are no porta-potties or restrooms at the Califon end, although there is usually a porta-potty at the township park in High Bridge. This trail has beautiful scenery with lots of food choices once you get into High Bridge.

RIDE DETAIL

This is the most scenic ride on the Columbia Trail. There are several parking options in Califon, the easiest being the old train depot. The trail goes south, paralleling Raritan River Road until the first road crossing, Hoffman Crossing. A little further south, the trail enters the Ken Lockwood WMA, which just does not seem like a part of New Jersey. There are no homes. The road is dirt. And, except for the fishermen along the river below, you are completely alone. After about 2 miles, you cross the river and road on an enclosed bridge. My kids refer to this as the "dinosaur bridge" since it reminds them of the birdcage in *Jurassic Park III*. There is a trail down to the river and road at this spot. It is steep but well traveled and a good spot from which to access the river.

Bridge crossing in Ken Lockwood WMA.

After another mile or so, you reach Cokesbury–High Bridge Road, which is crossed on a smaller, open bridge. Continue another half mile into High Bridge. Stay on the trail through the side streets in town, some of which are the trail and provide parking. The residents use the path for hiking and dog walking so you may have company on a weekend or nice summer evening. Directly across from the trail end at CR 513 is a small township park. For restaurants and shops, ride south (there is a sidewalk) a block or so on Main Street.

There are two loops possible using this end of the Columbia Trail but both use River Road for the return. With a junior biker, it is much better to do your return on the trail. River Road is paved for the first mile south of Califon and then turns to dirt/gravel through the WMA.

HOFFMAN'S CROSSING. Go south from the old Califon train depot on the trail. About 1.5 miles south, the trail intersects Hoffman Crossing Road. Turn left and return to Califon on River Road for a nice 3-mile loop.

KEN LOCKWOOD WMA. Go south from the old Califon train depot on the trail. About 2.5 miles south, the trail enters the Ken Lockwood WMA. In the gorge, when you reach the enclosed bridge, it is possible to access River Road again. It is a steep, slippery, downhill trek and just barely doable by walking the bikes. It is probably not possible with carts. Return to Califon on River Road. This is about a 5-mile loop.

WHERE TO START

From I-78, take Exit 17 and follow Route 31 north. Make a right (northeast) onto CR 513. Follow the signs carefully through High Bridge and continue on toward Califon. From CR 513, make a right (east) onto CR 512 (Main Street). After the big metal bridge in town, take the right fork, which is still CR 512, to the old train depot.

ALTERNATE PARKING

If you want a longer ride south to High Bridge or perhaps a shorter ride north to Long Valley, park at the small gravel parking lot on W. Valley Brook Road. Stay on CR 513 past Califon and make a right (east) onto Vernoy Road. Cross the bridge and go a short block on W. Valley Brook Road. The lot has space for a few cars. Starting from here lengthens the roundtrip to High Bridge to 14 miles and shortens the roundtrip to Long Valley to 8 miles.

If you want to start in High Bridge, take Exit 17 from I-78 and follow Route 31 north. Make a right (northeast) onto CR 513 toward High Bridge. Stay on CR 513 under the railroad and then make a left. The township park is a half mile north of town. The trail begins opposite the park, across CR 513.

FLANDERS

FOOD, FUN, AND RESTROOMS

Restaurants are plentiful along Route 206 in Flanders. For more options, head north from Flanders on Route 206 for about 4.5 miles. Make a right onto Gold Mine Road. There are several restaurants in this shopping complex, including a Macaroni Grill, Texas Steakhouse, and Chili's. If you continue on this road, you reach Route 46 where it intersects I-80.

SUBWAY AND MCDONALD'S. Both are in the A&P shopping center on Route 206 in Flanders.

AFTER CHAR-BROIL. This is a small local grill and ice cream shop about a mile north of Flanders on Route 206.

KENNEDY'S PUB. Casual, full-service restaurant located at the south end of the Route 206 Mall (across from the golf complex).

LONG VALLEY

A large portion of Washington Township, which consists of Long Valley and Schooley's Mountain, may have been America's earliest summer resort. The pure mountain air, romantic surroundings, and mineral springs attracted people to the area around the turn of the century. Originally known as German Valley, the town was renamed Long Valley during World War II. Today, this is a quiet little town with antique stores and several very good restaurants. For more choices, including typical fast food restaurants, travel east on CR 513 into Chester.

FOOD, FUN, AND RESTROOMS

LONG VALLEY PUB AND BREWERY. This restored mill is now a microbrewery and restaurant with outside dining on the patio. It is located on CR 517 a short block south of the CR 513 intersection.

ED & MIKE'S. If you are the curious type, take a minute to explore this antique and second-hand store. They have quite a collection of stuff, things, and whatevers for sale.

VALLEY RESTAURANT. This casual restaurant is in the strip mall on CR 513.

OLD MILL TAVERN. About 4 miles back toward Chester, this casual restaurant is located on CR 513, directly across from Cooper Mill.

SCHOOLEY'S MOUNTAIN PARK. This Morris County park, built on the site of the old YMCA Camp Washington, has picnic areas, ball fields, a small playground, hiking trails, and a small lake with paddleboat rentals. To find the park, follow CR 517 north and make a right onto Camp Washington Road. Follow the signs for another mile to the park. Do not try to bike this. CR 571 is twisty, steep, and has no shoulder.

HACKLEBARNEY STATE PARK. This park has picnic tables and hiking trails with some great rock climbing along the Black River. To find the park, go east on CR 513, make a right onto State Park Road, and follow the signs.

APPLE CIDER MILL. This working cider mill sells apple cider and baked goods. Kathleen recommends the cinnamon doughnuts! It is open from early September to late December. On busy fall weekends, there is also a hot dog vendor, corn maze (fee charged), and pumpkin patch. The mill is on State Park Road, about a mile before Hacklebarney State Park.

CALIFON

This town was originally named California to honor the investment of Jacob Neighbor's gold rush money. Legend has it that when the train station sign was painted in 1870, the name did not fit on the sign so the town was simply renamed Califon. That very same train station now houses the Califon Historical Society. Several of the local businesses are housed in buildings that date from the American Revolution or the Victorian era. All in all, Califon is a quiet little town and it is easy to bike around on side roads or on the sidewalks along Main Street.

FOOD, FUN, AND RESTROOMS

CALIFON FINE FOODS. This deli has delicious sandwiches, hot and cold salads, baked goods, and a variety of drinks. It is on Main Street, one block south of the trail. It is closed evenings and Sundays.

GREEN ONION. This café is located on CR 512, about a mile north of the trail. It is easy to bike to using sidewalks and, although the ride is uphill, it is not steep (one Kevin moan and one Kathleen groan). Indoor seating and restrooms are available.

BAGELSMITH. This deli has bagels, sandwiches, chips, snacks, drinks, etc. It is on CR 513 about one block west of the CR 512 inter-section. Restroom available.

MCDONALD'S. The nearest McD's is on Route 31, just before I-78. Take Main Street west to CR 513 and go south to Route 31. There is also a McDonald's about 4 miles north on Route 31.

MELICK'S ORCHARD. This farm stand has fruits, vegetables, and pick-your-own apples and peaches. It is on CR 513 just east of Califon. Look for a big red barn and deer fencing along the road. Porta-potties are usually available.

HIGH BRIDGE

This township has a long history, dating back to the early 1700s, when it was known as West New Jersey. During the American Revolution, a local ironworks cast cannonballs for the army, and a homestead on Lake Solitude was used to "house" John Penn, the last colonial governor of Pennsylvania. The forge was reopened in 1851 when the New Jersey Central Railroad line arrived. The town was named after the 1300-foot-long, 112-foot-high bridge built by the railroad to cross the South Branch of the Raritan River. The bridge was replaced in the mid-1860s by an embankment that still exists just south of town at Arch Street. Today, the town is better known for Voorhees State Park and the Ken Lockwood WMA, considered by many to have the best fly fishing in New Jersey.

FOOD, FUN, AND RESTROOMS

There are multiple restaurants in High Bridge and even more on Route 31, a few miles out of town.

CAFÉ AT ONE MAIN. Deli and coffeehouse serving breakfast and lunch in an informal café setting located at the end of Main Street, near the train depot. It is about three blocks south of the park. Closed Sundays and Mondays.

MICHAEL'S PIZZA. This small, take-out pizzeria is on Main Street.

GRONSKY'S MILK HOUSE. This classic ice cream stand with a fast food menu is located on Main Street about a mile south of the trailhead. Do not try to bike this. Main Street has considerable traffic and no sidewalks once you cross under the railroad bridge.

SUNSET INN. This is a casual, family-style restaurant on Route 31. From Califon, take CR 513 west and then go north on Route 31. The restaurant is within sight on the left. There is a patio available for outside dining.

VOORHEES STATE PARK. Besides picnic, playground, and camping areas, this state park has hiking trails and an observatory. It is on CR 513 about a mile north of High Bridge. Do not try to bike to this park. Traffic on CR 513 is heavy and moves quickly. Restrooms are available.

8

Black River Wildlife Management Area

COUNTY: Morris

TOWN: Chester

TYPE: out-and-back

RIDE DISTANCE: 8 miles

SURFACE: packed cinder

USAGE: Young Biker, Preschooler

RIDE SUMMARY

The rail-trail through the Black River Wildlife Management Area (WMA) is flat with a smooth, packed cinder surface. It travels through the hardwood forest along the Black River. There is nothing in the WMA—no roads, no houses, no restrooms, no porta-potties. It is probably the quietest, least-used trail we have ever found. After the solitude of the woods, a visit to Chester balances the day out nicely.

RIDE DETAIL

This trail is a designated portion of Patriots' Path and is a typical rail-trail with a hard, packed cinder base. It is built on the old right-of-way for the Chester Branch of the Delaware Lackawanna & Western Railroad, which ran 10 miles from Chester to Dover. It was

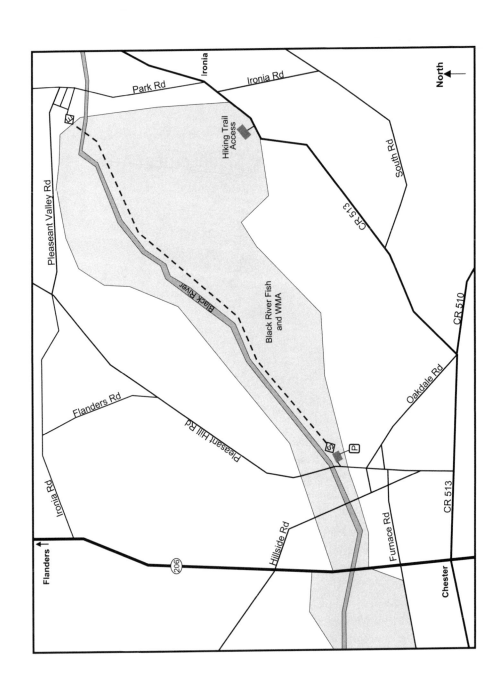

North

Ironia

Park Rd

Ironia Rd

Hiking Trail
Access

South Rd

Pleaseant Valley Rd

CR 513

Black River

Black River Fish
and WMA

Oakdale Rd

CR 510

Flanders Rd

Pleasant Hill Rd

Ironia Rd

Flanders

206

Hillside Rd

Furnace Rd

CR 513

Chester

constructed to move iron ore from the local mines to the furnaces and foundries in Dover. A large section, encompassing the wetlands around the Black River from Chester to Ironia, became part of the Black River WMA in 1965. WMAs are maintained by the New Jersey Division of Fish and Wildlife. Although their primary use is for hunting and fishing, these are wonderful areas for bird watching, hiking, wildlife photography, and, of course, biking. All WMAs are open to hunting in the fall and winter so please be very careful when planning this trip (go somewhere else in the fall). March to mid-September is best as these months have few or no hunting seasons, or pick a Sunday. Hunting is not allowed on Sunday in New Jersey.

The Morris County Patriots' Path map shows this trail running from Ironia to Cooper Mill, on the west side of Chester. Unfortunately, the trail system to the west of Route 206 is unsuitable for family biking. Just east of Chester, closer to Route 206, the trail is overgrown and unimproved. Thus, the best (well, only) section suitable for bikes is east of Pleasant Hill Road, heading toward Ironia. The surface was more grass than packed cinder in the first quarter mile but improved quickly. From the parking lot the trail goes northeast through the woods and ends behind some houses south of Ironia. There are no loops possible due to the amount of traffic on CR 513 (Dover–Chester Road). For current trail conditions, check with the Morris County Park Commission at www.parks. morris.nj.us or call 973-326-7600.

After your bike ride, drive back into Chester to explore the shops, eat lunch or ice cream, enjoy the local parks, or visit Cooper Mill. Do not bike into Chester. The roads get very congested with weekend shoppers and visitors.

WHERE TO START

From I-80, take Exit 27 to Route 206 South. In Chester at CR 513/Route 124, make a left (east) and then make the first left onto Hillside Road. At the fork, bear right onto Pleasant Hill Road. The gravel parking lot is on the right about a mile north—look for the Patriots' Path sign.

Black River near Chester.

CHESTER

In the mid-1700s, two roads crossed in what is now downtown Chester. These "grate" roads, one from New Brunswick in the south and one from Morristown in the east, allowed farmers to move their agricultural goods, including flax, wool, cattle, applejack, and peach whiskey, to market and get staples back. By the early 1800s, Chester Township was an important stagecoach stop on both these roads. In 1810 The Publick House, which is still operating as an inn and restaurant, opened to accommodate wealthier travelers. The town's first industry came in the mid-1800s with the construction of gristmills on the Black River. For a short time, seven mills operated on the Black River between Cooper Mill to the north and the Hacklebarney Mill to the south. Then in 1875, with the accidental discovery of iron ore by a local man digging an icehouse foundation, Chester became a boomtown with over thirty mines. Unfortunately, or fortunately, depending on your perspective, within ten years cheaper ore was found in Minnesota. By 1888 the mines and furnace were shut down and Chester returned to a quiet, little country town.

FOOD, FUN, AND RESTROOMS

Today, this area still offers travelers a place to rest and relax. Chester has excellent restaurants, several choices for fast food, over a half mile of specialty shops, and several great parks. When planning this trip, please remember that many of the shops and restaurants close on Mondays.

THE PUBLICK HOUSE. This is a restored country inn with a full-service restaurant on the corner of CR 513 and Hillside Road in Chester.

DAIRY QUEEN. On CR 513 in Chester, the DQ is a block from Route 206. The easiest place to park is behind the shops in the next block.

OLD MILL TAVERN. This is a casual, full-service restaurant located on CR 513 about a mile west of Route 206. It is directly across the street from Cooper Mill.

CHUBB PARK. This township park has a pond, tennis courts, hiking trails, and a large playground. Porta-potties are scattered about. It is located on CR 513 approximately a half mile west of Route 206.

ALSTEDE FARM MARKET. Local farm market with baked goods, fresh fruit, vegetables, plants, and lots of pet farm animals that can be hand fed—food, not fingers! It is on CR 513 across from Chubb Park.

Cooper Mill, near Chester.

COOPER MILL. Nathan Cooper built this gristmill in 1826. It was Cooper who incorporated the innovative designs of inventor Oliver Evans. With Evans' unique modifications, the Cooper Mill could produce 800 pounds of flour per hour. At its top speed of about 8 rpm, the wheel produced 45 horsepower. Although it weighs six tons or more, the wheel can be turned with as little as two cups of water per bucket! Today, Cooper Mill is a Morris County Park and the gristmill has been restored to working condition. In fact, stone-ground flour and meal can be purchased there. The mill is open Wednesday–Sunday from April to November, with special demonstrations of period crafts and skills throughout the summer and fall. Free. Restrooms are available. It is on CR 513 a mile west of Route 206.

APPLE CIDER MILL. This working cider mill, which sells apple cider and all kinds of baked goods, including cider doughnuts, pies, and breads, is good fun. Kathleen recommends the cinnamon doughnuts. It is open from early September to late December. To find the cider mill, continue on CR 513 past Cooper Mill. Make a left onto State Park Road and follow the signs toward Hacklebarney State Park. The mill is on your right.

RIAMEDE FARM. Visit this farm to pick your own apples on over 50 acres of apple trees and woods and get in a hayride as well. It is located on Oakdale Road near the CR 510 intersection. For more information on apple picking in the fall, call 908-879-5353.

Liberty Walk.

9

Liberty State Park

COUNTY: Hudson

TYPE: loop

RIDE DISTANCE: 4 miles

SURFACE: pavement

USAGE: Young Biker, Junior Biker, Preschooler, Toddler

RIDE SUMMARY

Liberty State Park is a small oasis in an industrial area. The park contains extensive picnic areas, wetland marshes, a first-rate playground, and miles of biking and walking trails. It is where the ferries leave for Ellis Island and Liberty Island, and it is the home of the Liberty Science Center. With so much to do, why bike? Because the bike trails are wonderful! Most are pavement or smooth brick and a good portion of the ride is along the water. And there are restrooms and food vendors everywhere. Of course, it is very popular and can be packed with visitors on weekends.

RIDE DETAIL

Liberty State Park, located on the Hudson River in Jersey City, is jam packed with fun things to do. With so much to see and do, you should choose your starting point carefully. If you are combining

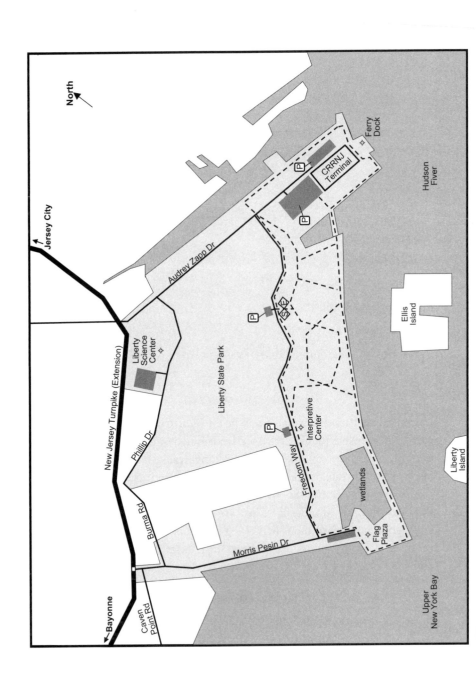

North

Jersey City

Bayonne

New Jersey Turnpike (Extension)

Caven Point Rd

Burma Rd

Phillip Dr

Liberty Science Center

Audrey Zapp Dr

Liberty State Park

Morris Pesin Dr

Freedom Way

Interpretive Center

wetlands

Flag Plaza

CRRNJ Terminal

Ferry Dock

Hudson River

Ellis Island

Liberty Island

Upper New York Bay

this ride with a trip to Ellis or Liberty Island, then use the parking lot at the Central Railroad of New Jersey (CRRNJ) terminal. There is a five-dollar parking fee, but it is good for the whole day. This also puts you close to the two restaurants in the park. If you are combining this ride with a visit to the Science Center, use the free parking area (two-hour limit) to the east of the CRRNJ terminal for your ride. Then drive back to the Science Center. The bike path does not go there. If you are just biking, park on Freedom Way in the middle of the park. This parking area, which is directly across the street from the playground and restrooms, only has space for about thirty cars but parking is free.

No matter where you start, make one of your stops the Interpretive Center. This building has a few simple, hands-on displays for kids (both the large and small variety) and park maps. Just north of the Flag Plaza, the path intersects Morris Pesin Drive, at which point the bike path disappears and you must ride on the road. It is not really a problem; Morris Pesin Drive is only used by park rangers in this area.

There are several places in the park to access Liberty Walk, which is a brick path along the Hudson River linking the CRRNJ terminal and the Flag Plaza. There are plenty of benches and stopping points along this 1-mile stretch. You can also zigzag through the park or loop back to your car. The whole area is flat and you will have to work really hard to get lost! With the views of the New York skyline, kite fliers in the park, the ships along the Hudson River, and, of course, the playground, we looped around for about 4 miles. For more information, visit the New Jersey Parks Division website www.state.nj.us/dep/parksandforests/ or www.libertystatepark.org or call 201-915-3400.

WHERE TO START

From the NJ Turnpike (I-95), take Exit 14B. After the tollbooth, make a left onto Morris Pesin Drive. Go straight at the traffic circle and then make a left onto Freedom Way. Go past the Interpretive Center to the parking area for the playground/picnic area. It is on your left.

ALTERNATE PARKING

If you want to use the CRRNJ terminal as your starting point, go left around the traffic circle onto Burma Road, which becomes Phillip Drive. Pass the Liberty Science Center and then make a right onto Audrey Zapp Drive. There is a large parking lot at the end of the CRRNJ terminal. A daily fee is charged. The parking area to the east of the terminal is free but there is a two-hour time limit. You can pick up a park map inside the terminal.

FOOD, FUN, AND RESTROOMS

Besides being a great place for an old-fashioned picnic, there are almost always food vendors scattered around the park, selling water, soda, Italian ices, and ice cream. There is a large vendor who sells more substantial kid-fare, like hot dogs, pretzels, and fresh fruit, near the ferry line. And there is a full-scale concession stand near the Flag Plaza. Please note that grilling is not allowed in the picnic areas.

LIBERTY PARK RESTAURANT. This full-service restaurant, with some outdoor dining on the patio, is located at the end of Liberty Walk and the marina parking lot.

LIGHTSHIP BAR & GRILL. This restaurant is on the big red lightship, close to the marina. Seating is available outdoors, weather permitting. This is a bit more casual than Liberty Park Restaurant.

LIBERTY SCIENCE CENTER. Located on Phillip Drive, this family-oriented science museum has three floors of interactive exhibits focusing on inventions, health, and the environment. There are separate admission charges for the museum and IMAX Theater. For more information, go to www.lsc.org or call 201-200-1000.

LIBERTY ISLAND. Lady Liberty was a gift to the United States from the people of France. It was commissioned to celebrate the two countries' friendship, founded during the American Revolution, and to commemorate the centennial of the American Declaration of Independence. Designed by Frederic Auguste Bartholdi, the statue and its pedestal in New York Harbor took ten years to complete. The statue was shipped to America, reconstructed, and opened to the public in October of 1886 by President Grover Cleveland. The ferry takes you to either or both of the islands and one charge covers both islands and all exhibits. A visit to the Statue of Liberty still requires quite a bit of stair climbing but there are lots of overlooks to enjoy along the way. For more information, visit the National Park Service website at www.nps.gov/stli/ or call 212-363-3200.

ELLIS ISLAND. Though a decade late, the Statue of Liberty was ready to welcome the millions of immigrants that flooded into the United States in the early 1900s. The current estimate is that over 12 million entered the country through the Ellis Island Immigration Station. On April 7, 1907, it processed an all-time high of 11,747 people. That year alone saw 1,004,756 new arrivals. Many then passed through the CRRNJ terminal to continue their journey to a new home. The ferries go to both islands for one fee. For more information, visit the National Park Service website at www.nps.gov/elis/ or call 212-363-3200.

Entrance sign for the park.

10

Duke Island Park

COUNTY: Somerset

TOWN: Somerville

TYPE: loop

RIDE DISTANCE: 3 miles

SURFACE: pavement

USAGE: Young Biker, Junior Biker, Preschooler, Toddler

RIDE SUMMARY

Take an afternoon (or morning) and explore the paved paths and canal towpath in Duke Island Park. The paved path loops through the woods parallel to the river and then swings back past the duck pond, ball fields, and playground. The canal and towpath travel through the middle of the park. The park can be crowded on weekends but most of the time this is just a quiet spot along the Raritan River. Restrooms are available at the visitor center.

RIDE DETAIL

This Somerset County Park is used for soccer games, competitive dog events, picnics, fishing, hiking, dog walking, and biking. The county acquired the 336-acre site in 1958. It truly is an island, with

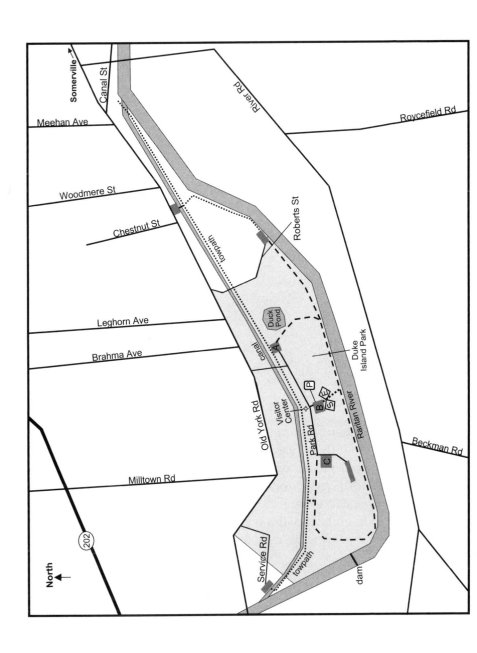

Somerville →

Canal St

River Rd

Roycefield Rd

Meehan Ave

Woodmere St

Chestnut St

towpath

Roberts St

Duck Pond

Leghorn Ave

canal

A

Duke Island Park

Brahma Ave

Old York Rd

Visitor Center

P

B

E

Raritan River

Beckman Rd

Park Rd

C

Milltown Rd

202

Service Rd

towpath

dam

North ←

the majority of the park located between the Raritan Power Canal and the Raritan River. The visitor center, which is located in the center of the park at Parking Lot B, houses the park office and public restrooms. Occasionally, there are porta-potties at the other parking lots. This seems to depend on the activity schedule.

Between the park loop and the canal towpath, there are lots of possible rides. The simplest starts at the visitor center and goes west (toward Parking Lot C) along the park road. If you happen to be in the park on a busy day and there is traffic on the road, ride the towpath. The easiest access point for the towpath, which is packed cinder in this section and very smooth, is right behind the visitor center. Once you pass Lot C, the trail enters the woods and begins a long, gentle curve south toward the river. It then parallels the river for the length of the park. At the east end of the park, the trail goes in two directions. One path goes north toward the duck pond and then wraps around to join the park road at Parking Lot A. The other path continues along the river for a little bit to Roberts Street. At the end of the Roberts Street parking lot, you can continue on the dirt trail but it does not really go anywhere.

The Raritan Power Canal and towpath run through the park and continue east another mile or so to the edge of Raritan. The towpath ends at the intersection of Canal Street and Old York Road. If you brave this narrow (2-feet-across) towpath, with its exposed roots and inconveniently spaced trees, the roundtrip adds about 2 miles. If you are just looking to extend your ride and explore, the towpath is in much better condition at the west end of the park near the dam.

WHERE TO START

From I-287, take Exit 17 for Routes 202 and 206 South toward Somerville. Where Routes 202 and 206 split, take Route 206 South toward Princeton. Go a half mile and make a right onto Somerset Street. Continue on through the small town of Raritan, where Somerset Street changes to Old York Road. Duke Island Park is on the left.

SOMERVILLE

FOOD, FUN, AND RESTROOMS

There is very little right around Duke Island Park since it is located between neighborhoods. A short ride to the east takes care of this problem nicely. Go east for 2.5 miles on Old York Road, whose name changes to Somerset Street in Raritan. Continue across Route 206 into Somerville. From Somerset Street, turn right onto Veterans Memorial Drive and use the Downtown Somerville Shopping Center for parking.

ALFONSO'S. A full-service Italian restaurant located in the middle of town, close to the Somerset County Courthouse.

MAIN STREET BISTRO. Located about a block west of the courthouse on Main Street, this eat-in deli/restaurant is another good choice.

CONE CENTRAL. This ice cream shop is on Main Street directly across from the central walkway in Downtown Somerville.

BASKIN-ROBBINS. This ice cream shop is in the middle of Downtown Somerville.

COUNTRY FRESH RESTAURANT. Located in Downtown Somerville with an entrance on Main Street, this deli/restaurant has outdoor tables.

SUBWAY. Also located in Downtown Somerville.

McDONALD'S. The McD's is on the far side of the Downtown Somerville parking lot.

U.S. BICYCLE HALL OF FAME. Somerville is the home of the bicycle racing hall of fame. The museum has bicycles, equipment, race stories, and other memorabilia from all of racing's great riders. It is located in the middle of Downtown Somerville. For more information, go to www.usbhof.com or call 908-722-3620.

WALLACE HOUSE. John Wallace, a Philadelphia merchant, purchased this house in 1775. He had just finished his renovations when George Washington secured the house as his headquarters for the winter of 1778. Martha Washington, aides, and servants also moved in during the Middlebrook Encampment. This house is one of the best examples of Georgian architecture in New Jersey. It is located in Somerville just east of the Route 206 and Somerset Street intersection. Hours vary by season so please call ahead: 908-725-1015.

TGI FRIDAY'S. Located in the shopping center at the intersection of Routes 206 and 202, a couple of miles north of Somerville.

11

Landsdown Trail

COUNTY: Hunterdon

TOWN: Clinton

TYPE: out-and-back

RIDE DISTANCE: 3.6 miles

SURFACE: packed gravel

USAGE: Young Biker, Junior Bike, Preschooler, Toddler

RIDE SUMMARY

The Landsdown Trail travels through hardwood forest and open fields along the South Branch of the Raritan River from Landsdown to Clinton. With a smooth, packed gravel surface, no road crossings, and no houses, this flat rail-trail is a quiet, well-hidden treasure in Hunterdon County. There are no facilities—restrooms or porta-potties—at either end, but the quaint little town of Clinton has a lot to offer.

RIDE DETAIL

This trail is part of the South Branch Reservation, which encompasses over 1,000 acres of parks and preserved wetlands in Hunterdon County. It is a rail-trail on what was once a spur line for the Lehigh Valley Railroad. This short section of track, which connected

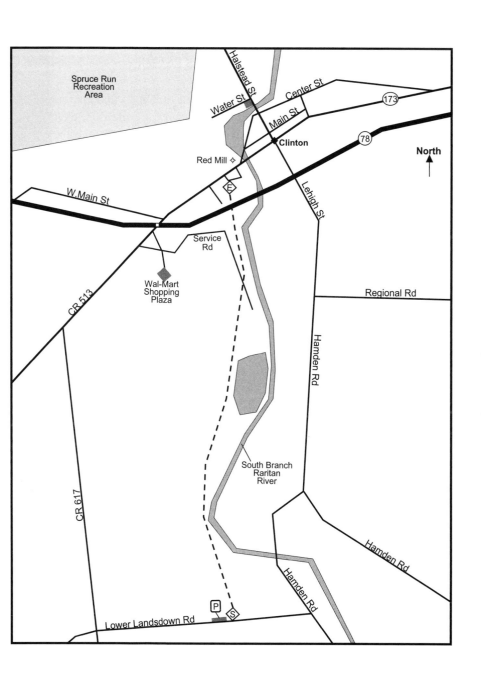

Spruce Run
Recreation
Area

Halstead St

Water St

Center St

Main St

173

Clinton

78

North

Red Mill

W.Main St

Lehigh St

Service
Rd

Regional Rd

CR 513

Wal-Mart
Shopping
Plaza

Hamden Rd

South Branch
Raritan
River

CR 617

Hamden Rd

Hamden Rd

P S

Lower Landsdown Rd

Clinton and Landsdown, was primarily a passenger line when it was completed in 1881. Some freight was also hauled over the line from Mulligan's Mill, which is now the Clinton Red Mill and the cornerstone of Clinton's downtown area.

Unfortunately, parking in Clinton can be difficult. Public parking is limited to the lots on the north side of town and a few side streets. It is easier to park along Lower Landsdown Road and bike back into Clinton, making this a bike out–eat lunch–bike back ride! The surface along the trail is packed gravel so the ride is fast and easy. The trail ends in the parking area for the Cyrus Fox Lumberyard. Cross the parking area and head for the main road (Route 173). This puts you across from the Clinton House at the end of Main Street, which is one-way, making for easy biking. There are also sidewalks, though narrow. Since all the restaurants and shops are within two blocks of the Clinton House, we park the bikes near the trail end and walk around town. The trail is 1.8 miles, making this a 3.6-mile roundtrip. There are no loops possible due to the amount of traffic on Hamden Road and Lehigh Street. For current trail information, go to www.co.hunterdon.nj.us/depts/parks/parks.htm or call 908-782-1158.

WHERE TO START

From I-78, take Exit 15 and go east on CR 513 (also Route 173) toward Clinton. At the first stoplight, make a right (south) onto Lehigh Street, which changes to Hamden Road outside of town. After a mile or so, Hamden Road bears right. (Please note that Hamden Road also goes straight—go figure.) From Hamden Road, make a right onto Lower Landsdown Road. Once past the church, you will see the start of the trail. There is space along the road for a half dozen cars.

CLINTON

Clinton is a charming little town along the South Branch of the Raritan River. It has several blocks of specialty shops, restaurants, and the famous Red Mill. It was in the 1750s that David McKinney built the first set of mills on opposite banks of the river, and the mills, in turn (no pun intended), drew other businesses to the area. The Red Mill was built around 1810 by the Mulligans to process wool, and later grain, plaster, graphite, and talc. In 1908 the roofline was extended to accommodate new machinery. It is this expansion that gives the mill its distinctive look. The bridge, which overlooks the 200-foot waterfall that separates the two mills, was constructed in 1870.

Red Mill in Clinton.

FOOD, FUN, AND RESTROOMS

RED MILL MUSEUM VILLAGE. With the mill, schoolhouse, trade buildings, and the Mulligan Quarry, the Hunterdon Historical Museum chronicles more than 180 years of county history. The village also hosts concerts, antique shows, craft fairs, and living history reenactments that frequently spill over into town. Kathleen still talks about the "marching band" that she saw on Main Street a few summers ago. The regiment marching across the bridge toward us was quite a sight. The village is open from early April to mid-October daily except Monday. Admission is charged. For more information, go to www.theredmill.org or call 908-735-4101.

HUNTERDON MUSEUM OF ART. Located in the Stone Mill, the art museum has approximately twelve exhibitions per year of local artists ranging from traditional to cutting edge. Open all year. Closed Monday. Free.

CLINTON HOUSE. This restored country inn opened in 1743, offering travelers on the South Branch of the Raritan River food and lodging. Today, travelers can still enjoy a meal in the restaurant on the corner of Main Street and CR 513.

PIZZA COMO. This pizzeria has lots of inside seating and is located on CR 513, about a block east of the Clinton House. Look for the narrow path between buildings to navigate between Main Street and W. Main Street.

OLD RIVER HOUSE. Located at the base of the bridge and offering dining on the patio, this restaurant has a lot to offer besides a traditional American menu.

TOMATO CAFÉ. This restaurant is a little more upscale. It is located on Main Street about half way up the block.

J. J. SCOOPS. Look for the small white building at the opposite end of Main Street from the bridge. This little ice cream store has limited patio seating out back.

MCDONALD'S. The closest McD's is at the corner of Route 31 and Center Street, about 2 miles east of town.

SPRUCE RUN RECREATION AREA. This state park offers three picnic areas, playgrounds, hiking trails, camping, and swimming in the reservoir, which covers 1,290 acres and has 15 miles of shoreline. It was the first water supply facility built by the state and is the third largest reservoir in New Jersey. From Clinton, go north on Halstead Street (also CR 513). At the stoplight on Route 31 make a left (north). There are park signs on Route 31 directing you to the main entrance, which is on Van Syckels Corner Road. A daily use fee is charged during the summer months.

12

Hoffman Park

COUNTY: Hunterdon

TYPE: loop

RIDE DISTANCE: 3 miles

SURFACE: pavement, packed gravel

USAGE: Young Biker, Junior Biker, Preschooler

RIDE SUMMARY

Hoffman Park is located just south of I-78 in the middle of Hunterdon County. The trails that crisscross the park are old roads with surfaces that vary from new pavement to crushed gravel. It is easy to ride loops and impossible to get lost. Most of the trails are flat and easy to bike except for the very first trail from the main parking area. Hairpin Lane is a steep downhill ride into the main area of the park, where there are about 2 miles of trails. We zigzagged and looped around and ended up biking about 3 miles. The biking is short and easy but there is not much else to do here unless you are into pond fishing! The main parking area off Baptist Church Road does have a porta-potty.

RIDE DETAIL

This 353-acre county park has hardwood forests, grasslands, and numerous ponds of various sizes. It is the former farm of the

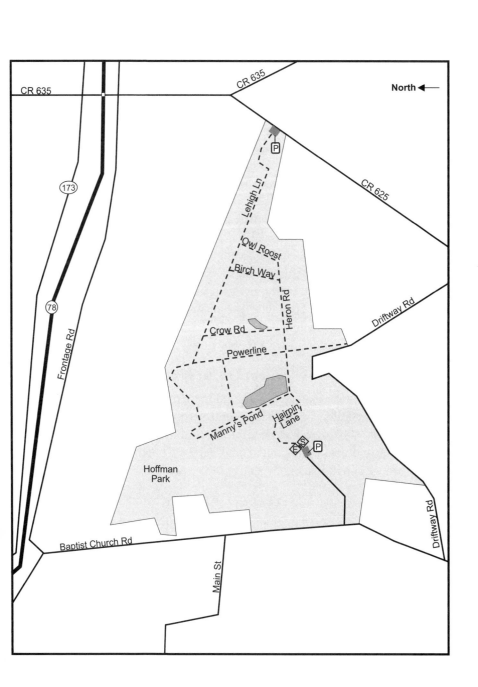

Hoffman family, who owned the Hoffman Beverage Company. Most of the Hoffmans' farm buildings still stand and are under the juris-diction of Union Township. Most of the trails are old farm roads except Hairpin Lane. It is a steep downhill ride to Manny's Pond, and the trip back up was a chore (major moaning and groaning). The rest of the park was easy riding with a few mild ups and downs over the 2 miles. This park is a good place to take a beginning biker or test out new equipment. For current trail information, go to the Hunterdon County Parks website, www.co.hunterdon.nj.us/depts/parks/parks.htm or call 908-782-1158.

The bike paths and a few frog ponds are the main attractions of this park. Manny's Pond and the pond on Crow's Road are large enough for fishing if you bring equipment. We did not bring nets or poles, so this trail is now officially Kevin's "least favorite" aka "never again!" Kathleen was riding her own bike for the first time, so her opinion was quite favorable. The main parking area contained a map stand and one lone porta-potty. For food and points of inter-est, it is necessary to drive a ways.

WHERE TO START

From I-78, take Exit 11. Go around the circle to the left and cross over I-78, following the signs for Pattenburg. Immediately after crossing I-78, turn left at the light. Proceed to the remains of an old church and turn right (south) onto Baptist Church Road. The park entrance is well marked by a large brown sign.

ALTERNATE PARKING

If you want to avoid the hill on Hairpin Lane, use the parking area on CR 625 (Mechlin Corner Road). This small, grassy lot has space for about ten cars and allows you to access the trail system via Lehigh Lane.

FOOD, FUN, AND RESTROOMS

Clinton is the closest town of any size. There are several other food and fun choices in the area but only a few and none are particularly close. This is primarily a rural area with horse and dairy farms—much like central Sussex County.

SPRUCE RUN RECREATION AREA. This state park has three picnic areas, playgrounds, hiking trails, camping, and swimming in the reservoir. Take Route 173 east to Route 31, then go north 2 miles and watch for signs. A daily use fee is charged during the summer months.

PERRYVILLE INN. This is a full-service restaurant with a traditional American menu located on Perryville Road (CR 635). Go south onto Driftway Road to get around the southern edge of the park and then go north on CR 625. The restaurant is at the intersection of CR 625 and Perryville Road.

PITTSTOWN INN. A restored county inn located in Pittstown, this full-service restaurant is about 4 miles away. Take Baptist Church Road south to Route 579 and follow into Pittstown. Parking for the inn is across the street in the gravel lot.

CRACKER BARREL. This family-friendly restaurant is located just off I-78 at Exit 15. Take Frontage Road east and follow signs for Wal-Mart. The restaurant is on the opposite side of the complex.

CLINTON HOUSE. This restored country inn opened in 1743, offering travelers on the South Branch of the Raritan River food and lodging. Today, travelers can still enjoy a meal in the restaurant, located in Clinton on the corner of Main Street and CR 513.

OLD RIVER HOUSE. You will find this restaurant at the base of the bridge on Main Street in downtown Clinton. Outdoor dining is offered during the summer.

J. J. SCOOPS. Located in a small white building in downtown Clinton at the far end of Main Street, this little ice cream store has limited patio seating out back.

MCDONALD'S. The closest McD's is at the corner of Route 31 and Center Street, about 2 miles east of Clinton.

13

Delaware & Raritan Main Canal

COUNTIES: Somerset, Mercer

TOWN: Griggstown

TRAIL DISTANCES
  Total Length 30 miles
  Landing Lane Bridge to South Bound Brook 5.3 miles
  South Bound Brook to Zarephath 3.1 miles
  Zarephath to Amwell Road 2.7 miles
  Amwell Road to Griggstown 5.6 miles
  Griggstown to Kingston 5 miles
  Kingston to Millstone Aqueduct 2.3 miles
  Millstone Aqueduct to U.S. Route 1 6 miles

The idea for a canal across New Jersey dates back to 1676, when William Penn authorized surveyors to consider the possibility of a canal from the Delaware River to New York Bay. It took another 150 years before construction actually began. The Delaware & Raritan Canal and Camden & Amboy Railroad companies obtained canal and railroad charters in 1830. The companies combined in 1831 and by 1834 the Delaware & Raritan (D&R) Canal opened for through traffic at a cost of $2.83 million. The D&R Canal consisted of two sections, which formed a V across the state of New Jersey. The main canal ran from New Brunswick to Trenton, a distance of 44 miles. The feeder canal ran from Raven Rock to Trenton, a distance of

22 miles. The D&R Canal quickly became one of America's busiest. Its peak decades were the 1860s and 1870s; in 1866 nearly three million tons moved through the canal. During this time, the main cargo was coal, traveling from the mines in Pennsylvania to the industrial furnaces of New York City.

With only fourteen locks overcoming an elevation change of 115 feet, the canal was fairly simple compared to the Morris Canal. The D&R, however, had several design advances and, like the large transportation systems of today, it was constantly being upgraded with new technology and innovations. The D&R was constructed with "swing bridges," allowing vessels with high masts through, since the canal was a link in the inland waterway. So a vast variety of boats traveled the canal, from coal barges to sailboats to steam tugs to millionaires' yachts. In 1846 a telegraph line was installed along the canal to expedite boat traffic, control water flow, and catch ships speeding over the allowed 4.5-mph speed limit. In 1847 outlet locks were added at Wells Falls, just south of Lambertville, so canal boats could pass across the Delaware River via cable ferry to the Delaware Canal. In 1853 the banks of the canal were rip-rapped—lined with stone—to allow ships to travel at a reasonable speed without eroding the banks. By 1858 the locks were expanded to 220 feet and the bridges were enlarged sufficiently to allow two boats to pass at one time. With all the improvements, prizes and bonuses were offered to encourage greater speed on the canal but by 1893 the canal was operating at a loss. Decades of decline followed until the canal, towpath, and few remaining structures were reclaimed as historic landmarks and the Delaware & Raritan Canal State Park was created.

In our pre–kid era, we rode this towpath and ended up with structural damage to both our bodies and bikes. The roots, ruts and wet spots combined for some really rough riding. Thankfully, the D&R State Park has fixed all these problems and more. The trail is now a smooth packed cinder from start to finish. Unlike some of the canal rides along the Delaware River where parking is at a premium, you can do this ride anytime. With thirteen easy-to-find parking areas, you can relax and plan the trip your way. And, while restrooms

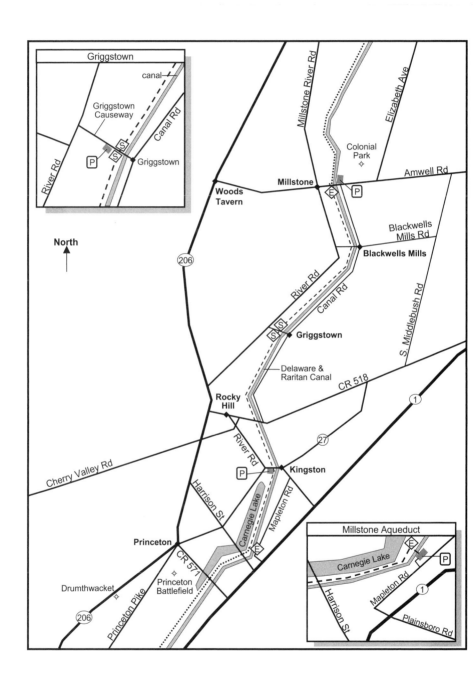

Griggstown

canal

Griggstown
Causeway

Canal Rd

River Rd

P S

Griggstown

North

Millstone River Rd

Elizabeth Ave

Colonial
Park

Amwell Rd

Millstone

P

(206)

**Woods
Tavern**

Blackwells
Mills Rd

River Rd

Canal Rd

Blackwells Mills

S. Middlebush Rd

S

Griggstown

Delaware &
Raritan Canal

CR 518

**Rocky
Hill**

27

1

River Rd

Cherry Valley Rd

P

Kingston

Mapleton Rd

Harrison St

Carnegie Lake

Princeton

CR 571

Drumthwacket

Princeton Pike

Princeton
Battlefield

(206)

Millstone Aqueduct

Carnegie Lake

Mapleton Rd

P

1

Harrison St

Plainsboro Rd

are still scarce, there are porta-potties in many of the parking lots. With so many starting points, the ride options are almost endless, so I selected two, both starting from Griggstown. For current trail conditions, visit the D&R Canal State Park website at www. dandrcanal.com or call 732-873-3050.

GRIGGSTOWN TO AMWELL ROAD RIDE

COUNTY: Somerset
TOWN: Griggstown
TYPE: out-and-back
RIDE DISTANCE: 11 miles
SURFACE: packed cinder
USAGE: Young Biker, Junior Biker, Preschooler, Toddler

RIDE SUMMARY

If you are just getting started, this is a great first choice. This canal ride always seems much shorter than 11 miles, and it is hard to believe you are riding through one of the most densely populated areas of New Jersey. The trail has a smooth, packed cinder surface and runs between the canal and the Millstone River. There is only one road crossing, at Blackwells Mills Road.

RIDE DETAIL

We typically start at Griggstown since it has a large parking area and is relatively easy to find from Route 206. From the parking lot on Griggstown Causeway, the towpath is immediately visible as you approach the wooden bridge. You do need to cross and then walk along the Griggstown Causeway for a short distance. With the Griggstown boat rental just across the bridge, there are frequently canoes and kayaks on the canal through the first mile or so. The towpath goes north 3.5 miles from Griggstown to Blackwells Mills, where there is usually a porta-potty in the parking lot. Although Blackwells Mills is a "town," there is not much here. After you cross Blackwells Mills Road, it is a swift 2-mile ride to Amwell Road, along which the towpath parallels Canal Road until just before Millstone.

Like Blackwells Mills, there is not much in Millstone. Turning around here makes the roundtrip about 11 miles.

If you continue north, it is another 2 miles to the Weston Causeway. There is a large parking area caddy corner to the towpath entrance. With this extension, the roundtrip ride from Griggstown is just under 15 miles. North of the Weston Causeway, the towpath runs 3 miles before the next access at South Bound Brook Road and another 5 miles or so to its end at Landing Lane Bridge. This northern section, with its highways, old warehouses, and industrial buildings, is not as nice to ride through as further south.

WHERE TO START

From I-287, take Exit 17 for Route 202/206 South. In Somerville where the two roads split, take Route 206 South toward Princeton. After 10 miles or so on Route 206, make a left (east) onto River Road. Go 1 mile north and make a right (east) onto Griggstown Causeway. The parking area is on your right, a short block before the canal bridge.

ALTERNATE PARKING

If you want to start in Millstone (not to be confused with the Millstone Aqueduct, which is near Princeton) and ride south to Griggstown, from Route 206 South make a left (east) onto Amwell Road. Make a left (north) onto Millstone River Road and then a right onto Millstone Causeway. The parking area here has space for thirty or more cars.

GRIGGSTOWN TO MILLSTONE AQUEDUCT RIDE

COUNTIES: Somerset, Mercer
TOWN: Griggstown
TYPE: out-and-back
RIDE DISTANCE: 14 miles
SURFACE: packed cinder
USAGE: Young Biker, Junior Biker, Preschooler, Toddler

RIDE SUMMARY

From Griggstown south to Princeton is a lovely ride and one of my favorites. The smooth, packed cinder surface makes this a fast, easy ride that takes you through Rocky Hill and Kingston. These are some of the most popular biking and hiking trails in the area, but crowding is not a problem as the parking lots are large and all have porta-potties. The only road crossing is in Rocky Hill since there is an underpass for Route 27 in Kingston.

RIDE DETAIL

This middle section of the D&R Main Canal offers great biking, and there are numerous options for food and fun. When starting from Griggstown, we never worry about parking, although you must walk along Griggstown Causeway a short distance to get on the trail. For the length of this ride, the canal is sandwiched between the Millstone River and Canal Road, which is very popular with street bikers. With several local stables, there are frequently equestrians on the trail here—along with the ever present Canada geese!

Canada goose on the canal.

It is 3 miles south to Rocky Hill, where you must cross CR 518. The town of Rocky Hill is a half mile or so to the west and uphill. Since for Kevin and Kathleen, hills are definite no-no's on canal rides, we always continue on to Kingston, which is just under 2 miles further south. As you approach Kingston, you may see hikers on the opposite side of the canal in the Cook Natural Area. At Route 27, the towpath passes under the road and continues past the parking area and one of the five remaining locks on the D&R. The town of Kingston is several blocks to the east and also somewhat uphill.

Lock at the Millstone Causeway.

From Kingston to the Millstone Aqueduct, the towpath runs parallel to Carnegie Lake for the majority of the 2 miles. This is one of the nicest sections along the towpath, with the canal on one side, the lake on the other, and no roads to be seen. It is also loaded with wildlife. Kevin and Kathleen frequently "detain" young painted turtles in this area. The turtles do not seem to mind the inspection process and they get a safe, free lift from one side to the other. At the Millstone Aqueduct, the Millstone River heads off southwest while the canal continues to parallel Carnegie Lake. It is just over 7 miles from Griggstown to the Millstone Aqueduct, making the roundtrip about 14 miles.

The Millstone Aqueduct is a picturesque spot but does not provide access to Princeton. If you continue south for a half mile, the canal intersects Harrison Street, and another half mile south is Washington Road (CR 571). A mile west on either of these roads puts you in downtown Princeton. While this is feasible with a child in a bike seat, it is difficult and dangerous with kids on their own bikes or with a cart. It is also too far to walk. Just south of Washington Road, the canal crosses Alexander Road and then continues for several miles to Port Mercer, where it crosses Quaker Bridge Road. If you ride this far south, the roundtrip to Griggstown is almost 24 miles.

WHERE TO START

From I-287, take Exit 17 for Route 202/206 South. In Somerville where the two roads split, take Route 206 South toward Princeton. After 10 miles or so on Route 206, make a left (east) onto River Road. Go 1 mile north and make a right (east) onto Griggstown Causeway. The parking area is on your right, a short block before the canal bridge.

ALTERNATE PARKING

If you want to start at the Millstone Aqueduct (not to be confused with the town of Millstone) and ride north to Griggstown, from Route 1 South take the exit for Mapleton Road. If you are northbound on Route 1, this is the Plainsboro Road exit. Look for the parking area on your left after a half mile or so on Mapleton Road.

GRIGGSTOWN

Griggstown is in Franklin Township, which was settled in the early 1700s by the Dutch, who saw quite a bit of action right on their doorsteps during the Revolutionary War. After the Battle of Princeton, General Washington and the Continental Army withdrew along the Millstone River and camped overnight in Millstone. Later that year, the British forces under Generals Cornwallis and DeHeister camped in East Millstone and Middlebush. Griggstown was also the home of John Honeyman, a successful American spy. Posing as a cattle trader sympathetic to the British, he penetrated the British forces and obtained information that helped Washington plan the surprise attack that liberated Trenton. Though it figured large in local history, Griggstown remained small until sixty years later, when the D&R Canal was built. Some of the canal structures have been preserved near the Griggstown bridge, including a bridge tender's house, mule tenders' barracks, and the site of the Griggstown mill. The Griggstown lock is a mile south along the canal, where picnic tables and grills are available.

FOOD, FUN, AND RESTROOMS

D&R CANAL MUSEUM. This is located in the old mule tenders' barracks. In the mid-1800s mule tenders were almost always children, some as young as nine years old, and they either slept outside or on the boat. On the D&R Canal, there were facilities for children in Griggstown, Bordentown, and one more in the middle. When the boats began to use steam power, the barracks were converted into stores, homes, or post offices. Museum hours vary. Admission is free.

GRIGGSTOWN CANOE AND KAYAK RENTAL. Located on the Griggstown Causeway at the base of the wooden bridge, this privately owned shop has both canoes and kayaks for rent. The canal north of Griggstown can be quite colorful with all the canoes and their occupants in bright orange safety vests. For more information, call 908-359-5970. Open weekends.

CARVEL ICE CREAM. This popular ice cream shop is north of Woods Tavern on Route 206.

MCDONALD'S AND BURGER KING. You can find both of these and a few other fast food places on Route 206 just north of the Amwell Road (CR 514) intersection.

CHARLIE BROWN'S. This restaurant is located in the same vicinity as the fast food favorites on Route 206.

COLONIAL PARK. This 650-acre facility is a Somerset County Park. There are several large picnic areas and elaborate playgrounds. Several ponds are stocked yearly and paddleboat rentals are available on Powder Mill Pond. The main park entrance is on Mettlers Road, a half mile east of the Millstone parking area.

GOOD-TIME CHARLEY'S. The only way we can get the kids to ride uphill on a canal ride is for this restaurant. It is in Kingston, which is indeed uphill from the canal, but there are sidewalks and it is only two blocks. It is a casual, family-friendly place and the ride back to the canal is all downhill!

RUBY TUESDAY. You cannot miss this one. It is on the corner of Mapleton Road and Route 1 South. Since it is on the curve of Mapleton Road, it is possible to bike to this restaurant from the Millstone Aqueduct parking lot. It is less than a half mile of road riding and you can use Lakeview Terrace to avoid riding part of Mapleton Road.

CARNEGIE LAKE. A little-known early use of the D&R Canal was for practice by the Princeton rowing team. By the 1880s, however, canal traffic was so heavy that rowing had become dangerous. So in 1902 a former rower, Howard Butler, approached his friend, Andrew Carnegie, for funds to flood a large swampy area between Kingston and Princeton, thus creating a lake for rowing races and training. Carnegie agreed and put up $450,000 for a 3-mile-long lake. Completed in 1906, the lake, fed by the Millstone River and Stony Brook Creek and controlled by the north end dam, reached a water level of 12 feet. Today, there are houses along the western shore but lake access for boating and fishing is possible from the Millstone Aqueduct and Kingston parking areas.

PRINCETON BATTLEFIELD STATE PARK. On January 3, 1777, the fields and woods around Princeton exploded with gun and cannon fire as the Continental Army clashed with British troops. The Clarke House, built by Thomas Clarke in 1772, saw some of the fiercest fighting and served as a sanctuary for General Mercer, who died there nine days later from multiple bayonet wounds. It is possible to access the park from the towpath if you continue past the end of Carnegie Lake and head toward the Alexander Road parking lot. By car from Route 206, take Lovers Lane east to Mercer Street and turn right (south). This becomes Princeton Pike. The park is open daily and the Clarke house is open Wednesday through Sunday.

DRUMTHWACKET. This is the official residence of the Governor of New Jersey. Tours through the mansion, including the six public rooms used by the Governor for meetings, are available every Wednesday morning. Reservations are required and must be made one week in advance. For more information, go to www.drumthwacket.org or call 609-683-0057. From the Millstone Aqueduct parking area, go out to Route 1 and then south to CR 571 (Washington Road). Go west toward Princeton on CR 571. Make a left on Route 27 (Nassau Street) and then take Route 206 South (Stockton Street). Drumthwacket will be on your left a quarter mile past the light at the Elm Road intersection.

14

Sandy Hook National Recreation Area

COUNTY: Monmouth

TYPE: out-and-back

RIDE DISTANCE: 10 miles

SURFACE: pavement

USAGE: Young Biker, Junior Biker, Preschooler, Toddler

RIDE SUMMARY

Built in 2004, this paved recreation trail runs 5 miles down the length of Sandy Hook, part of the Gateway National Recreation Area. The path runs from the park gate to the tip of Fort Hancock, where it does a small loop past Officer's Row and other historic buildings. Each beach access point has a restroom and there are almost too many historic sites on the peninsula to visit in one day. The only tough part of this ride is the wind, which seems to blow right at you in both directions! Bring lunch or plan to return to the Highlands since there is only one fast food restaurant in the park.

RIDE DETAIL

Sandy Hook, a 1,665-acre barrier beach peninsula, is the northern tip of the New Jersey shore. With 7 miles of beaches, the waters of

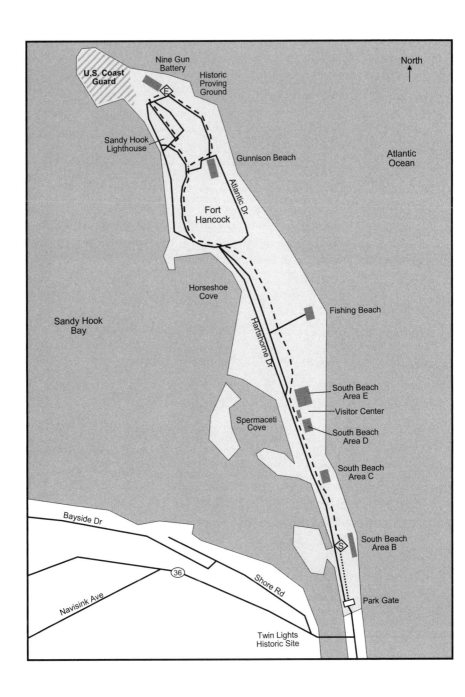

North

U.S. Coast Guard

Nine Gun Battery

Historic Proving Ground

Sandy Hook Lighthouse

Gunnison Beach

Atlantic Ocean

Atlantic Dr

Fort Hancock

Horseshoe Cove

Sandy Hook Bay

Hartshorne Dr

Fishing Beach

South Beach Area E

Visitor Center

Spermaceti Cove

South Beach Area D

South Beach Area C

Bayside Dr

South Beach Area B

36

Shore Rd

Navisink Ave

Park Gate

Twin Lights Historic Site

Sandy Hook Bay, salt marshes, dunes with prickly pear cactus and hermit crabs, and 264 acres of maritime forest dotted with American Holly, this has long been a recreation area popular with beach goers, naturalists, and bird watchers. Now it is also a biker's paradise. The paved path is so wide they painted a yellow line down the middle to separate the lanes, and it connects all the unique spots and historic sites in the park.

Once you are in the park (yes, there is a fee for parking—this is a National Park), the first parking lot is South Beach Area B. For maximum riding, this is where you want to park. For the first mile or so the trail runs parallel to and fairly close to Hartshorne Drive, but strategically located sand dunes prevent you from feeling like you are riding "on the road." Please use extra caution when crossing the beach access roads. Most drivers are focused on finding a parking spot—not looking for bikers. South Beach parking areas D and E flank the visitor center, which has very clean, indoor restrooms. For the next 2 miles, the path weaves through the woods until it reaches the base of Fort Hancock.

At the fort entrance, the path goes in a loop. Cross Hartshorne Drive and follow the path past Officer's Row to the Sandy Hook Lighthouse. The bike path continues around to the east side of the peninsula, passing the Nine Gun Battery, Proving Ground, and Gunnison Beach. There are many other small roads in Fort Hancock going this way or that. Traffic is generally light so it is safe to explore. Back at the fort entrance, the loop road rejoins the main path, which allows you to return south. For current trail information, go to www.nps.gov/gate or call 732-872-5970.

WHERE TO START

The only safe place to begin this ride is inside Sandy Hook Park. From the Garden State Parkway, take Exit 117. Go east on Route 36. It is about 13 miles to the bridge at Sandy Hook Bay. Follow the signs into the park, which charges a daily (or annual) parking fee for most of the year. The South Beach Area B parking lot is on the right.

Riding the path at Sandy Hook.

FOOD, FUN, AND RESTROOMS

There have been forts on Sandy Hook, guarding the entrance to New York Harbor, since the late 1700s. The British built the first defenses during their occupation of New York during the Revolutionary War. During the War of 1812, it was the United States military that occupied the peninsula, but it was not until the 1890s that the military established a permanent presence on Sandy Hook. In 1891 construction began on new concrete defenses, and new gun batteries soon followed. By 1899 a large section of the main post was complete and the base was named Fort Hancock in honor of Civil War General Winfield Scott Hancock. For the next half century, defenses at Fort Hancock were constantly upgraded with new technology, and during the 1950s it became one of the sites where the military installed Nike surface-to-air missiles. Finally, in 1974 the Army base was decommissioned and Fort Hancock became part of the National Park Service's Gateway National Recreation Area.

FORT HANCOCK MUSEUM. Sandy Hook became the home of Fort Hancock in 1899 when the first thirty-four buildings were completed, including eighteen Georgian Revival–style homes for officers and their families. Throughout the next century, Fort Hancock was armed with the most sophisticated weaponry of the day. The peninsula was actually home to two different branches of the U.S. Army. The Artillery Corps garrisoned at Fort Hancock was charged with protecting New York Harbor, while the Proving Grounds were used to test or "prove" new weapons for the Army's use. A temporary proving ground was established in 1874 near the north end, along the ocean. The firing range extended 3,000 yards along the beach or out to sea. In the early 1900s, the Proving Ground became an official permanent installation, and a locomotive storage house, machine shops, storehouses, and barracks were soon built. Their red brick distinguished the Proving Ground buildings from the buff-colored structures of Fort Hancock. The museum devoted to the story of Fort Hancock and

Sandy Hook is housed in one of the buildings dating from 1899. It is open afternoons—daily during the summer, otherwise just weekends. Admission is free.

HISTORY HOUSE. This restored home in Fort Hancock's Officers' Row is open weekend afternoons, year-round.

BATTERY POTTER. Also named after a Civil War officer, this battery, completed in 1893, was different from all previous weapon sites. First, it was located in a bunker made from thick concrete. Second, it was situated behind a large earthen mound, which hid the battery from the view of ships in the harbor. Third, its twelve-inch guns fired thousand-pound shells powerful enough to break through the thin armor on most warships of the time. Finally, the guns rode up and down on a steam-powered hydraulic lift. The elevator raised the gun to firing position and then lowered it for reloading. These "disappearing guns" required a huge bunker to house the boilers, coal storage, and other equipment needed to work the steam-powered lifts. Although the guns are long gone, the bunker remains and can be toured on weekend afternoons throughout the year. Admission is free.

SANDY HOOK VISITOR CENTER. Located in the middle of the park, the Visitor Center is the former Spermaceti Cove U.S. Life-Saving Station. In the late nineteenth century, shipwrecks on or near shore were common in New Jersey. In 1849, with funds provided by Congress, "lifeboat stations" were constructed at 10-mile intervals along the Jersey shore, from Sandy Hook to Long Beach Island. Each station housed rescue teams and their equipment. With the New Jersey stations as models, life-saving stations were soon established all along the Eastern seaboard and throughout the Great Lakes region. Leaving behind a splendid record of aiding 28,121 vessels and rescuing 178,741 persons, with only 1,455 lost lives, the Life-Saving Service merged with the U.S. Revenue Cutter Service in 1915 to create the United States Coast Guard. Today, the Sandy Hook Visitor Center is home to an exhibit honoring the men who served on this beach. Open daily.

SANDY HOOK LIGHTHOUSE. This is the oldest lighthouse still in use in the United States. The funds to purchase the land and construct the lighthouse came from the proceeds of two lotteries authorized by the New York Provincial Congress in 1761. Completed in 1764, the lighthouse was built about 500 feet from the tip of the peninsula. Today, due to the northward expansion of the peninsula, the

Sandy Hook Lighthouse.

lighthouse stands over a mile from the tip. In 1883 the lighthouse keeper was provided with a new home, which is the dwelling that stands today. The Sandy Hook lighthouse was the first in the country to be lit with electricity. It is still in active service, equipped with the original third-order Fresnel lens illuminated by a thousand-watt bulb, which is visible 19 miles out to sea. Tours are available weekend afternoons, except during the winter months.

SEA GULL NEST. This large concession stand offers lots of typical fast food and ample seating. Located at South Beach Area E, it is open only during the summer.

15

Hartshorne Woods Park

COUNTY: Monmouth

TYPE: out-and-back

RIDE DISTANCE: 4 miles

SURFACE: pavement

USAGE: Young Biker, Preschooler, Toddler

RIDE SUMMARY

Hartshorne Woods is a great little park for biking. Tucked away above the Twin Lights Historic Site, this Monmouth County Park has 16 miles of trails. The 5 miles of trails in the Rocky Point section are paved but none are flat. Most are not steep as much as long and arduous, though one or two qualify as leg-burners! The views, however, are worth the climb. Near the Rocky Point parking lot, there are a few picnic tables and a porta-potty.

RIDE DETAIL

Hartshorne Woods, a 736-acre park, has three sections: Buttermilk Valley, Monmouth Hills, and Rocky Point. The Rocky Point section was the Highlands Army Air Defense Site from 1940 to the mid-1970s. During World War II, the main battery housed two 66-foot-long guns, which were phased out in the 1950s. Some years later, Rocky

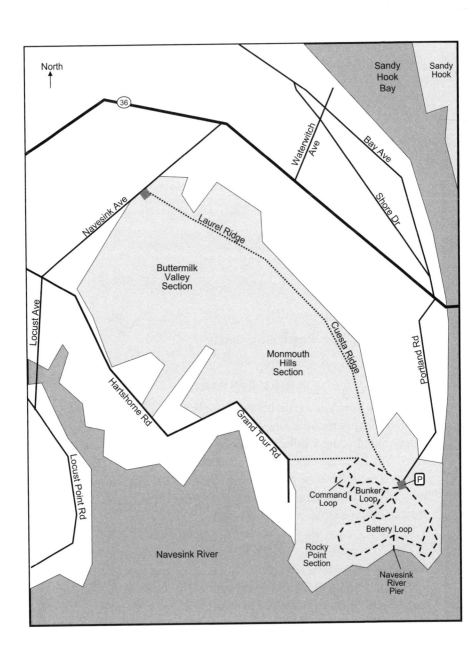

Point became a Nike-Hercules Missile Control Center. Eventually, the Army decided the area was surplus property and Monmouth County purchased the 224-acre site as an addition to Hartshorne Woods Park.

Each section of the park has its own trail system and many of the trails connect. We restricted our ride to Rocky Point since this area has paved trails. Starting from the parking lot, it is easy to do several loops. The Battery Loop is the longest at about 1.5 miles with a short side trip down (really, really down) to the Navesink River Pier. The Battery-Lewis Loop is very short but the kids loved going through the bunker tunnel and the views were spectacular. The Command Loop was a bit longer and can be combined with a side trip down to Grand Tour Road. Explore—you cannot really get lost but remember, every trail that goes down must come back up! We biked around all the loops, did some doubling-back, and ended up riding about 4 miles, which felt like more due to the hills.

For a longer ride, try the Cuesta Ridge Trail, which runs for 2 miles along the ridge through the Monmouth Hills and Buttermilk Valley sections. It is an old gravel road with a packed gravel surface and it rolls a bit—not steep hills but not flat either. The roundtrip is 4 miles or so. Cuesta Ridge ends at the Navesink Avenue parking area. For current trail conditions, go to www.monmouthcountyparks. com or call 732-872-0336.

WHERE TO START

From the Garden State Parkway, take Exit 117. Go east on Route 36. It is about 13 miles to the bridge at Sandy Hook Bay. Just before the bridge, make a right onto Portland Road and continue up the hill. The parking area, which has space for about twenty cars, is at the end of Portland Road.

FOOD, FUN, AND RESTROOMS

A unique park with its military flavor, Hartshorne Woods is fun to visit but there are no facilities and the surrounding area is suburban. Fortunately, the park is very close to the Highlands and Sandy Hook.

SANDY HOOK. This National Park is part of the Gateway National Recreation Area. It is a 1,665-acre barrier beach peninsula at the tip of New Jersey. Besides 7 miles of beach with multiple access points, the Sandy Hook Visitor Center is a former U.S. Life-Saving Station. The Sandy Hook Lighthouse is the oldest in the nation still in use. And Fort Hancock and its impressive gun batteries are open for tours. The park is open daily. Most of the museums are open weekend afternoons. For the entrance to Sandy Hook, go back to Route 36 and continue east over the bridge. Follow the signs into the park. There is a daily parking fee. For more information, go to www.nps.gov/gate or call 732-872-5970.

Battery Lewis tunnel.

NAVESINK TWIN LIGHTS. The Highlands of Navesink, rising 200 feet above sea level, were a natural location for a light station to aid navigation. The spot was used for signals as early as 1746 but it was not until 1828 that the federal government constructed permanent lighthouses. The first "twin lights" were two identical but separate towers. After some serious wear-and-tear, these were torn down and the existing complex was built with two towers connected by storage areas and keeper's quarters. Completed in 1862, the Twin Lights tower 250 feet above Sandy Hook Bay. The complex is open throughout the summer. Admission and tours are free. For more information, go to www.twin-lights.org or call 732-872-1814.

OFF THE HOOK. This full-service restaurant with a casual atmosphere is on the corner of Route 36 and Portland Road.

INLET CAFÉ. This casual, full-service restaurant is on Sandy Hook Bay in the Highlands. From Route 36, make a left onto Bay Avenue and then a right onto Shrewsbury Street.

WIND AND SEA. This slightly more formal restaurant is also on Shrewsbury Street.

TUGBOAT WILLY'S. This casual, full-service restaurant is also on Sandy Hook Bay in the Highlands. From Route 36, make a left onto Bay Avenue and then a right onto Marine Place.

CLAM HUT. This casual, full-service restaurant on Sandy Hook Bay in the Highlands has tables available outside. From Route 36, make a left onto Bay Avenue and then a right onto Atlantic Avenue.

MCDONALD'S AND BURGER KING. The nearest fast food restaurants are west on Route 36 about 4 miles.

16

Edgar Felix Bike Path

COUNTY: Monmouth

TOWN: Manasquan

TYPE: out-and-back

RIDE DISTANCE: 7 miles

SURFACE: pavement

USAGE: Young Biker, Junior Biker, Preschooler, Toddler

RIDE SUMMARY

The paved Edgar Felix Bike Path is a nice, easy ride. It sneaks between neighborhoods and through coastal forests, avoiding most roads in a very congested area. The map shows this trail crossing multiple roads, but a bike bridge across the Garden State Parkway and underpasses at Routes 34 and 35 eliminate the big ones, leaving only a few small roads to cross in Allenwood. Wheel, foot, and paw traffic is heavy on the trail, however, and we were often forced to go single file. There are restrooms close by in Allaire State Park and porta-potties at Orchard Park.

RIDE DETAIL

The bike path is built on the abandoned Freehold-Jamesburg Railroad, which was chartered in 1851 and commenced operations in

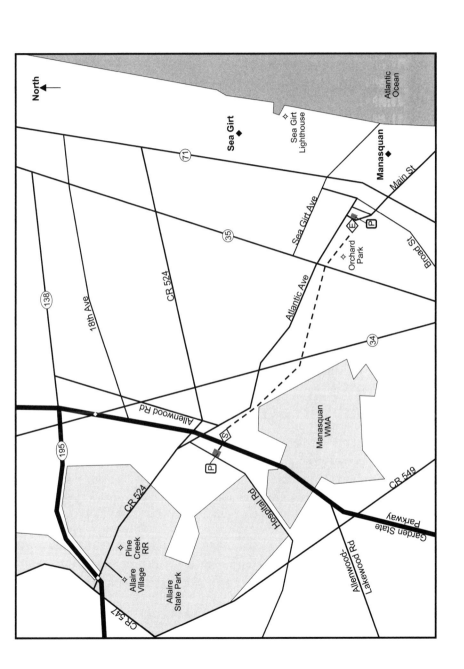

1853, carrying produce from local farms to city markets. The rail line ran from Freehold to Jamesburg, where it connected to the Camden & Amboy Railroad. Though the railroad line still remains, the trail is not marked west of Hospital Road, and the surface is grass. And there are detours around the Spring Meadow Golf Course, Allaire Village, and I-195.

The Edgar Felix Bike Path is the 3.5-mile section east of Hospital Road. It runs from Hospital Road, just outside Allaire State Park, to Manasquan, where the trail ends just north of the downtown area, providing easy access to shops and restaurants. There is a public parking area across the street if you want to park your bikes and walk through town. The path also passes through Orchard Park, which has a playground and porta-potties, just before Manasquan. This bike out–eat lunch–bike back trail gets high marks from the kids when we combine it with a visit to Allaire Village.

There are several areas where you do *not* want to ride:

To the Beach. Although Manasquan is within 2 miles of the beach, the streets closer to the beach are congested and narrow. The sidewalks are uneven and there are multiple dangerous intersections, including Route 71.

Allaire Village. Both Hospital and Allaire Roads have quite a bit of traffic and there are no shoulders. So riding to Allaire Village is a tad unwise. Furthermore, bikes are not allowed in Allaire Village.

Allaire State Park. This park offers miles of mountain biking trails, just minus the mountains. Unfortunately, the trails also present riders with lots of deep sand and nasty, exposed roots.

Where to Start

From I-95, take Exit 31. Go north on CR 547 (Lakewood–Farmingdale Road) for a short distance and then make a right (east) onto CR 524 (Farmingdale Road). Continue past the park and then make a right onto Hospital Road. Look for the small, unmarked gravel parking lot on your left.

ALTERNATE PARKING

If you want to start in Manasquan, take Exit 98 from the Garden State Parkway and follow Route 34 South. Make a left (east) onto Atlantic Avenue (CR 524 Spur) and continue into Manasquan. There is a municipal parking lot on Main Street, one block south of Atlantic Avenue.

ALLAIRE STATE PARK

This state park on New Jersey's outer coastal plain has over 3,000 acres of pine and oak forest similar to that found in the heart of the New Jersey Pinelands. The Manasquan River bisects the park and flows east into the Atlantic Ocean. In addition to the nature center and hiking trails, the park has several creeks, swamps and wetland areas. Fishing is allowed at the pond in Allaire Village and bamboo fishing poles can be rented at the Bakery. For more information, visit www.state.nj.us/dep/parksandforests/ or call 732-938-2371.

PICNIC GROUNDS. The largest picnic area and playground are to the right of the main parking lot. Well-maintained restrooms are located near the picnic grounds and in the brick building at the end of the parking lot. The picnic area, which provides grills and fire pits, is very popular and gets crowded on weekends and holidays. Although there are no restaurants within the park boundaries, there is usually a concession stand vendor located near the Pine Creek Railroad, providing typical "kid fare"—hot dogs, hamburgers, French fries, snacks, soda, and bottled water.

PINE CREEK RAILROAD. This railroad offers the only narrow-gauge, steam train ride in New Jersey. It is an example of the narrow-gauge railroads that helped to expand the American frontiers in the 1800s. Smaller-gauge equipment meant lower costs and easier construction in remote and mountainous regions. The steam locomotive, coach, and caboose are maintained just as they were when in regular service. Train rides are available from early April

Pine Creek Railroad steam engine.

to mid-October for a small fee. As you travel through the park, you can hear the train whistle blow!

ALLAIRE VILLAGE. Howell Iron Works (now Allaire Village) produced bog iron during the early 1800s. The self-contained community was established by James Allaire, a brass founder from New York City. Its four hundred or more inhabitants included workers with a variety of skills needed to run the iron furnace and serve the families who lived on the premises in brick row homes built by Allaire. With its own general store, carpenter shop, blacksmith shop, gristmill, bakery, church, and school, the village thrived for over thirty years.

Iron production flourished in this area of New Jersey. Deposited along riverbanks and in swamps, bog iron ore was mined and smelted from the 1760s into the mid-1800s. Inside the furnace, layers of charcoal, iron ore, and oyster or clamshells were alternated. The charcoal was then lit and the hot air blasted through the furnace. The ore melted and the shells filtered out impurities as the molten iron drained to the bottom, where it was poured into molds for weapons, pots, nails, and tools. The Howell Iron Works prospered until competition from the higher-grade ores from Pennsylvania began to reduce profits. The furnace was shut down in 1848 and the community began to decline. Today it is a restored nineteenth-century village. Many of the buildings are open to the public, with craftspeople giving demonstrations and providing historical background information. There is no fee to tour the village once you are in the park.

MANASQUAN

Manasquan was first settled in the late 1600s as a part of Shrewsbury. Its name originated from the Lenni Lenape Indians, who summered in the area. The Lenape name *Man-A-Squaw-Han* means stream of the island of squaws. Today, this small town has a "Main Street" atmosphere with a variety of shops and services. It is an easy ride into town on the sidewalk from the municipal parking lot.

Manasquan is also a popular seashore location with four parking lots for beach access. Badges are required and can be purchased at any beach entrance.

Food, Fun, and Restrooms

Allenwood General Store. Part antique store, part convenience store, part deli, and part bakery, this general store is on the bike path at the intersection of Atlantic Avenue and Ramshorn Road. There is a restroom, though you only want to use it in an emergency.

Dairy Queen. This ice cream shop is just around the corner, at the intersection of Main Street and Atlantic Avenue,.

The Foodery. Located in the Main Street Station shopping center, a mile southeast on Main Street (across Route 71), this restaurant is part deli, part coffeehouse.

Squan Tavern. This Italian restaurant serves lunch and dinner and is two blocks northeast on Broad Street.

O'Neill's Restaurant. With dining inside and outside on the porch, this restaurant is about a mile southeast on Main Street (across Route 71).

17

Manasquan Reservoir

COUNTY: Monmouth

TYPE: Loop

RIDE DISTANCE: 5 miles

SURFACE: packed cinder

USAGE: Young Biker, Junior Biker, Preschooler, Toddler

RIDE SUMMARY

The perimeter trail is a 5-mile loop through the woods and wetland areas around the Manasquan Reservoir. It is open to dog walkers, joggers, horseback riders, and bicyclers. The well-maintained surface is a packed cinder. The Joseph C. Irwin Visitor Center has ample parking and restrooms, while Chestnut Point has a small lot and porta-potties. This flat loop is a good choice for a beginner biker.

RIDE DETAIL

The Manasquan Reservoir, located in Howell Township, is the water source for Monmouth County. Construction began on the Timber Swamp Brook in 1987, and in 1990 the facility became operational, capable of supplying up to 30 million gallons of water a day. Water from the Manasquan River is pumped into the 770-acre reservoir

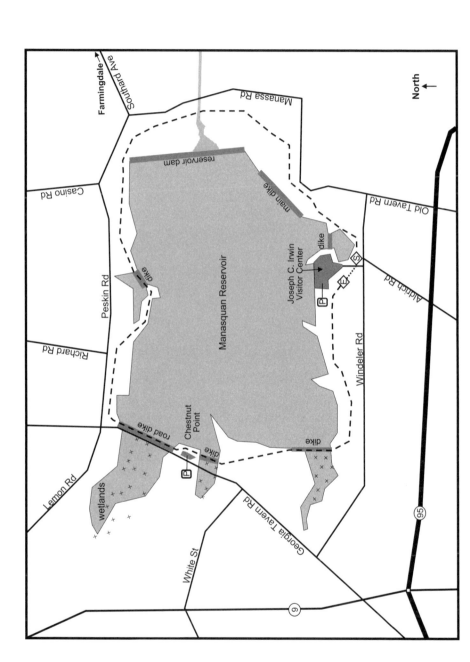

North ←

Farmingdale
Southard Ave
Manassa Rd
Casino Rd
Old Tavern Rd
reservoir dam
main dike
Peskin Rd
dike
Joseph C. Irwin Visitor Center
dike
Richard Rd
Manasquan Reservoir
Windeler Rd
Aldrich Rd
Chestnut Point
road dike
dike
dike
Lemon Rd
wetlands
Georgia Tavern Rd
White St
95
9

through a pipeline that is 66 inches in diameter and over 5 miles long. The reservoir is incorporated in the Joseph C. Irwin Recreation Area, which is operated by the Monmouth County Park System. The 1,200-acre park has woods, wetlands, a multi-use trail, fishing, boating areas, and a visitor center. Several sections of the park are designated wetlands, where all use is prohibited. Please note signs and stay on the trail in these areas. The park is open year-round and admission is free.

Use the visitor center as your base. It has clean, indoor restrooms and a food concession stand. From the west side of the parking lot, there is a short path to the perimeter trail, which eliminates riding across the parking lot. The perimeter trail crosses multiple dikes and bridges but only one road—the entrance to the visitor center! It parallels Georgia Tavern Road for a short distance at the western end of the reservoir, but the bike path is separated from the road by cement barriers. Although narrow and a little noisy, it is very safe. If you ride the loop counter-clockwise, you will pass the Chestnut Point parking lot, which has porta-potties, about 4 miles around. For current trail conditions, visit www.monmouthcountyparks.com or call 732-919-0996.

WHERE TO START

From I-95, take Exit 28 to Route 9 North. At the first stoplight, make a right onto Georgia Tavern Road. Make another right onto Windeler Road. The park entrance is well marked Or, for the easiest trail access, go to the left (west side) of the parking area.

FOOD, FUN, AND RESTROOMS

While there is not much around the park (it is kind of sandwiched between neighborhoods), a short ride to the east or west takes care of this problem nicely. To the east is the little town of Farmingdale. Continue around the reservoir, make a right (east) onto Southard Avenue, and continue to the intersection with CR 524. Or, for easy fast food and a variety of restaurants, go west on Windeler Road and then either north or south on Route 9.

JOSEPH C. IRWIN VISITOR CENTER. This includes a concession stand, which is open from late spring through October. Boat rentals (paddleboats and rowboats) are also available at the visitor center. During the summer, visitors may take a scenic tour aboard a large pontoon boat. The reservoir is stocked with bass, trout, tiger muskie, pan fish species, and bullhead catfish. Fishing licenses are only required for anglers older than fourteen. If you need one, day licenses can be purchased at the visitor center. Please note that there is no swimming allowed on the reservoir and there are no picnic areas.

Visitor Center.

TWO DIPS AND MORE. This ice cream store is in Farmingdale on CR 514, a few blocks south of the Southard Avenue intersection.

TONY'S PIZZERIA. If pizza is the choice of the day, take CR 524 south (right) in Farmingdale for about a quarter mile.

ICE CREAM ON 9. This ice cream shop on Route 9 is about a mile north of Georgia Tavern Road.

IVY LEAGUE. This full-service restaurant is on Route 9 at the corner of East Third Street.

MCDONALD'S. Go north on Route 9 about a mile.

BOSTON MARKET. Go south on Route 9, under I-95, to the Lakewood Shopping Center. There are other fast food choices available in this area.

Delaware River Bridge near Stockton, New Jersey.

18

Delaware & Raritan Feeder Canal

COUNTIES: Hunterdon, Mercer

TOWNS: Frenchtown, Stockton, Lambertville, Washington Crossing State Park

TRAIL DISTANCES
Total Length 34 miles
Milford to Frenchtown 3.5 miles
Frenchtown to Stockton 12 miles
Stockton to Lambertville 3.5 miles
Lambertville to Washington Crossing State Park 7 miles
Washington Crossing State Park to Trenton 8 miles

Constructed during the great canal era of the early 1800s, the Delaware & Raritan (D&R) Feeder Canal runs 22 miles down the western edge of New Jersey from Raven Rock to Trenton. Originally built to provide water for the main Delaware & Raritan Canal, the feeder canal was soon used for hauling also and saw heavy traffic from its first year. The feeder canal started at Raven Rock, the highest elevation of the Delaware River, and joined the main canal at the summit level in Trenton. From there, at 58 feet above sea level, the water flowed northeast to New Brunswick.

Canals did not operate during the winter, however, and so the Belvidere-Delaware Railroad was constructed in 1855 beside the feeder canal to haul coal during the winter months. Actually, the railroad tracks were laid on the towpath and a new towpath was built on the opposite side of the canal. This rail line ran over 30 miles from Milford to Trenton. The feeder canal and rail line remnants are now part of the D&R Canal State Park and provide some of the best biking in New Jersey.

While the majority of the bike path is on the rail-trail, the towpath is smoother in some sections due to its packed cinder surface. Both go to the same places so it does not matter which you ride. There are a few dead ends, though, so if you are exploring, be prepared to backtrack. There are multiple starting points and lots of place to park. Furthermore, many of the parking areas have restrooms and picnic areas, and porta-potties are scattered along the length of the canal. For current trail conditions, visit the D&R Canal State Park website at www.dandrcanal.com or call 732-873-3050.

If you cross into Pennsylvania, the bike path is the Delaware Canal towpath, which runs 60 miles from Easton south to Bristol, just outside Philadelphia. For more information on creating a loop, refer to chapter 20, Delaware Canal.

FRENCHTOWN TO STOCKTON RIDE

COUNTY: Hunterdon
TOWNS: Frenchtown, Stockton
TYPE: out-and-back
RIDE DISTANCE: 24 miles
SURFACE: packed cinder
USAGE: Young Biker, Preschooler

RIDE SUMMARY

Ready for a challenge? The ride from Frenchtown to Stockton is a 24-mile roundtrip, whole day excursion. Both towns have lots to offer in the way of food, shopping, and special events plus you travel through the Bull's Island Recreation Area and Prallsville Mills historic site. The trail has a smooth, packed cinder surface and parallels the Delaware River and Route 29. Although the trail runs very close to the road in some sections, the canal is between the road

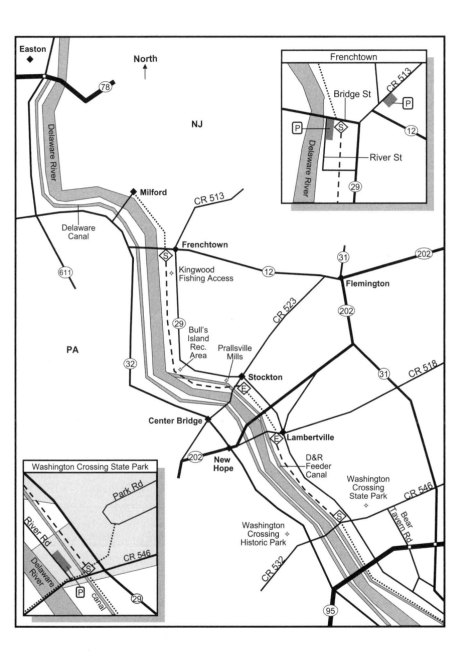

and trail. There are a few small road crossings, access roads for the houses along the river mostly, and several river access parking lots to navigate across.

RIDE DETAIL

The majority of this ride is on the old Belvidere-Delaware Railroad line since Frenchtown is several miles north of where the feeder canal begins at the Bull's Island Recreation Area. Needless to say, the Delaware River area is popular with trail riders, road riders and tourists exploring the canal, river, and town so start early! Do not wait until mid-day or parking and eating may be serious problems.

There are several starting points in Frenchtown. The easiest parking area is at the old railroad station, which is now the Bridge Street Café. There are about twenty-five parking spots here but the lot fills up quickly. The bike path is well marked and obvious from this parking area closest to the bridge. As you ride south out of town, there is one small road to cross at the edge of town. The next landmark is the Kingston Fishing Access and Boat Launch, which is about a mile south. From the boat launch south, the trail runs very close to Route 29 for another 8 miles before entering the Bull's Island Recreation Area, which is definitely worth a stop. The visitor center, with clean restrooms, picnic area, and playground, is just over the canal bridge. There is also a pedestrian bridge across the Delaware River to Lumberville, Pennsylvania. If you want to shorten your ride, cross here and ride north on the Delaware Canal towpath for a 16-mile loop back to Frenchtown.

Continuing south, you pass the Prallsville Mills historic site, which makes a nice rest stop with several buildings to explore, porta-potties, and a good place to toss stones into the Delaware River. It is only a mile further south into the small town of Stockton, where all the restaurants and shops are on Bridge Street.

WHERE TO START

From I-287, take Route 202 south into Flemington. At the circle, take Route 12 west to Frenchtown. Make a left onto Bridge Street. The parking area is on the left just before the bridge to Pennsylvania.

Alternate Parking

Another choice in Frenchtown is to use the public parking lot on CR 513. From Route 12, make a right onto CR 513 and look for the lot on your right. There are about fifteen spots. It is two blocks into town so this does not add much to your ride. If you have young bikers, walk your bikes through town.

If you want to shorten this trip a little, just south of Frenchtown on Route 29 is the Kingston Fishing Access and Boat Launch, which has lots of parking and is right on the towpath. Using this as your start point makes the roundtrip to Stockton about 12 miles.

If you want to ride north from Stockton, the best choice is to park at Prallsville Mills. Take Route 202 southwest until you reach the Delaware River (last exit in New Jersey) and then Route 29 north to Stockton. Continue through Stockton to Prallsville Mills, a mile north on the right. The towpath is easy to find. This also shortens the ride north to about 12 miles.

Washington Crossing State Park to Lambertville Ride

COUNTY: Mercer
TOWNS: Washington Crossing State Park, Lambertville
TYPE: out-and-back
RIDE DISTANCE: 14 miles
SURFACE: packed cinder
USAGE: Young Biker, Junior Biker, Preschooler, Toddler

Ride Summary

From Washington Crossing State Park, which has great facilities, including restrooms, picnic areas, playgrounds, and lots of parking, go north on the towpath to Lambertville. The towpath has a smooth, packed cinder surface with long sections in the open and very few road crossings. This is a fast, fun ride. It can be busy with other bikers and hikers, particularly at the southern end close to the park.

Bridge over the Delaware River.

It is about 7 miles north to Lambertville, making the roundtrip about 14 miles. Even better, you can modify the trip into a loop by returning on the Delaware Canal towpath in Pennsylvania.

RIDE DETAIL

The southern end of the Delaware & Raritan Feeder Canal is in Trenton where the feeder canal joins the main canal. Biking around the Trenton area, however, is not as nice as farther north. As you get closer to Trenton the canal moves away from the river and there are multiple road crossings.

A better option is to start from Washington Crossing State Park. There are multiple picnic areas with restrooms and playgrounds scattered throughout the park, and the park road is easy to ride southwest toward the river and canal. You pass the visitor center, several of the restored structures, and the monument. A pedestrian bridge over Route 29 puts you at the River Road parking and picnic area, which also makes an excellent choice for parking.

Regardless of how you get to the River Road picnic area, ride north on the towpath. Within the first mile and a half, there are four small road crossings for the houses along River Road, but after Church Street, there are only three access points along the remaining 5.5 miles to Lambertville. Stay alert in this area since there are occasional washout areas, leaving steep drops on the river side. Make sure children ride along the inside of the path or walk your bikes. The trail runs between the Delaware River and the D&R Feeder Canal until just south of Lambertville where you cross the canal. Lambertville has lots of shops and restaurants and, like New Hope, can be extremely crowded on summer weekends. Navigating the narrow, busy streets in Lambertville gives me nightmares, so we park our bikes near the canal and walk through town. This helps stretch out tired muscles and is safer for everyone.

If you want to make this ride a loop, cross the Delaware River into New Hope, Pennsylvania. Continue west for one block to the Delaware Canal towpath. You can go south on this towpath to the Washington Crossing Historic Park on the Pennsylvania side. This park has a lot to offer—more than the New Jersey side, including replicas of the Durham boats, a very nice visitor center, and an ice cream shop. Cross the bridge into New Jersey to return to the River Road parking area.

WHERE TO START

For the canal parking at Washington Crossing State Park, take Exit 2 from I-95. Go north on Bear Tavern Road and then make a left (west) onto CR 546 (Washington Crossing–Pennington Road). You will pass the park entrance road after about a mile. Continue on CR 546 and cross Route 29. Make a right on River Road just before the bridge to Pennsylvania. The parking area is on the right.

ALTERNATE PARKING

There are multiple picnic areas in the park, with ample space for parking. Most are at the northern end of the park. We rode the park road south, stopping at the visitor center and monument on our way to the canal trail. There is a pedestrian bridge over Route 29. On weekends during the summer there is a daily use fee.

If you want to start in Lambertville and ride south to Washington Crossing State Park, think again. There are very few public parking areas in Lambertville and street parking can be very hard to find. This is a great town, but not a good choice for starting a long bike ride.

FRENCHTOWN

One hundred years ago the population of Frenchtown was 1,545. Today, Frenchtown still has about the same number. This picturesque little town on the Delaware River is very similar to the village established in 1785 by Thomas Lowery, who built a gristmill and sawmill on the river. The area had several different names, including Sunbeam and Sherrod's Ferry, before the current name became permanent. "Frenchtown" came from a French-speaking immigrant, Mallet-Prevost, who settled in the area in the late 1700s.

The first small store in the town was a built around 1820. The first train came through town about 1853 on the Belvidere-Delaware Railroad line. The old railroad station, located next to the bridge, is now a café. For a very small town, there are a surprising number of choices for food, and most of the stores and restaurants are right on Bridge Street.

Food, Fun, and Restrooms

Bridge Street Café. This popular café on Bridge Street is across from the bridge and on the towpath. It is so popular with bikers that bike racks are provided.

Frenchtown Inn. This old, restored country inn is one block north of the bridge on Bridge Street and is a bit more formal than the other choices in town.

Market Café and Bakery. This café at the intersection of Routes 12 and 29 is also an ice cream shop.

Frenchtown Café. This small restaurant serves breakfast and lunch and specializes in cappuccino and espresso.

Galasso's Pizza. If pizza is the day's choice, this eat-in pizzeria is at the corner of Bridge Street and Route 29.

Buck's Ice Cream & Espresso Bar. If ice cream is what you are after, this shop is also on Bridge Street, one building north of the Route 29 turn.

Race Street Café. This is casual restaurant is tucked into the corner, just off Bridge Street.

River Crossing Café. This casual café is on Route 29 about a mile south of town. It is on the towpath and has lots of outdoor benches. On warm sunny days this is a particularly good choice since you will avoid the crowds in Frenchtown.

STOCKTON

This small river town has a long history, starting with the Stockton Inn, which began operations in 1710. It is home to Prallsville Mills, a small industrial complex built by John Prall in the late 1700s.

Stockton is also the home of the early inventor John Deats, who patented the iron plow in 1828. Deats's son Hiram had an iron furnace operating in Hunterdon County to manufacture the new plow in 1831, and by 1852 a branch factory was built in Stockton. Hiram Deats became the first millionaire in the county. Today, the area is known for country dining and shopping.

FOOD, FUN, AND RESTROOMS

ERRICO'S MARKET. Half deli and half store, this market has soda, water, baked goods, sandwiches, and ice cream bars. It is on the bike trail at the corner of Bridge and Railroad Streets. There are no public restrooms.

STOCKTON INN. This famous bed and breakfast has a full-service dining room, with outdoor seating in the summer. It is at the corner of Bridge Street and Route 29.

MEIL'S. This eat-in or take-out deli is caddy corner to the Stockton Inn.

DILLY'S CORNER. Another popular biking stop, this ice cream stand also has a complete fast food menu. It is in Center Bridge (just across the river from Stockton) at the intersection of Routes 263 and 32.

PRALLSVILLE MILLS. John Prall put this industrial complex together around 1794. The mills were used to make linseed oil and flour and to saw lumber. The second owners of the mills deeded property to the canal in the 1830s and to the railroad in the 1850s to ensure service for the mill complex. Take a journey back in time to the early 1800s and explore the gristmill, linseed oil mill, and sawmill. Porta-potties are available. The buildings are open on a limited basis. For more information, go to www.dandrcanal.com/prallsville.html.

BULL'S ISLAND RECREATION AREA. The "Big Ditch," as the canal was called during its construction from 1831 to 1834, was built by Irish immigrants using shovels, pick axes, and wheelbarrows. The pay was a dollar per day and the workweek was six days—Monday through Saturday. Many immigrants were fleeing worse conditions in Ireland and often had to work off the twelve-dollar passage and seventeen-dollar provision charge for the trip to America. Masons were paid more for bridge and lock construction, and some of the biggest, strongest workers received twenty-five dollars for tree stump removal. Tragically, many of the Irishmen died in the Asiatic Cholera Epidemic that swept through the canal camps in 1832. Legend has it that many were buried along the canal, under the towpath, and in nearby fields. Regardless of their burial sites, a large memorial was placed here to commemorate the

Prallsville Mills.

contributions of these men. The visitor center also has displays and information about the construction of the D&R Canal. There is ample parking, as well as restrooms, porta-potties, picnic grounds with a small playground, boat launch, wading areas along the Delaware River, and a pedestrian bridge across the river to Lumberville, Pennsylvania. It is on the towpath about 3 miles north of Stockton. For more information, visit the New Jersey Parks Division website at www.state.nj.us/dep/parksandforests/.

LAMBERTVILLE

This town has great restaurants and shops. It is also bigger than Frenchtown and Stockton, with four or five blocks of small specialty stores, delis, and intriguing cafés to explore. We park our bikes and walk, since the narrow sidewalks make it difficult to ride around town, and the traffic jams can rival those of New York City at rush hour!

FOOD, FUN, AND RESTROOMS

LILLY'S ON THE CANAL. Tucked away down a side street, this restaurant is on the canal (about a block off Bridge Street). The atmosphere is casual. This is also a good place to park bikes since it is off the main road.

BUCK'S ICE CREAM. There is a lot more than just ice cream here. Buck's is on Bridge Street about two blocks east of the bridge.

FULL MOON. This little restaurant serves breakfast and lunch and is located on Bridge Street just a block or so east of the bridge.

LAMBERTVILLE STATION RESTAURANT AND STATION PUB. The old stone train station offers two dining options. You cannot miss it—just before the bridge.

HOWELL LIVING HISTORY FARM. This sprawling estate has been a farm for over 250 years. The Mercer County park system restored the farm to its early twentieth century appearance, and it is now a living history farm with an hour and a half self-guided tour of orchards, fields, and pastures with sheep, ducks, geese, beehives, and much more. The farm also offers a full calendar of special events, including maple sugaring, workhorse rides, craft workshops, hayrides, sheep shearing, and even plowing. To find Howell Farm, which is halfway between Lambertville and Washington Crossing State Park, take Route 29 south out of Lambertville. Make a left onto Valley Road. After 1.5 miles, make a left onto Woodens Lane; the entrance road is a quarter mile on the right. For more information, visit www.howellfarm.org or call 609-737-3299.

WASHINGTON CROSSING STATE PARK

On November 21, 1776, General Washington's troops fled from Fort Lee barely ahead of the British army, led by General Howe. Washington moved south to Newark. Just seven days later, on November 28 as the British arrived, Washington left Newark, retreating to New Brunswick. After more troop losses and desertions, Washington's remaining three thousand men began the march to Princeton on December 1, again as the British advanced. Washington himself stayed in the rear, ordering the troops to cut down trees and burn bridges in an attempt to slow the British progress. Within a week, the entire Continental Army had retreated all the way to Trenton. On December 8, Washington sent his troops across the Delaware River. All the boats along the river for miles were confiscated and moved to the west bank. The Continental Army occupied the river from Dunk's Ferry to Coryell's Ferry, and all the crossings were carefully guarded. Howe believed Washington defeated and returned to New York, leaving Hessian troops guarding Trenton. And so, the stage was set for Washington's strategic battle—launched from Taylorsville, now known as Washington's Crossing.

Today, there are two state parks here—one on the New Jersey side and one on the Pennsylvania side—commemorating the site of the Continental Army's crossing of the Delaware River on December 24, 1776. While the parks both have a lot to offer, there are very few restaurants in the vicinity.

Food, Fun, and Restrooms

WASHINGTON CROSSING STATE PARK. This thousand-acre park in New Jersey preserves the landing site of the Continental Army on Christmas Eve in 1776, prior to the Battle of Trenton. There are several historic sites in the park. Continental Lane marks the old road used by the army in its march from the river. The Johnson Ferry House is set up to depict the life of a ferry keeper, and it is believed that General Washington and his officers used this house as a base while they waited for the army to cross the river. Another preserved building, the Nelson House, marks the landing site of the Pennsylvania ferry. The park also has a visitor center, monument, numerous picnic areas, and playgrounds. For more information, visit the New Jersey Parks Division website at www.state.nj.us/dep/parksandforests/.

FAHERTY'S. Located on Route 29 near the entrance to the bridge, Faherty's is half restaurant and half convenience store. It is quite obvious from the south end of the River Road parking area, but it can be a bit hard to reach when there is heavy bridge traffic.

TAYLORSVILLE STORE. On the Pennsylvania side, this small store has a variety of gifts, snacks, ice cream, and cold drinks. It is on Washington Crossing Road (CR 532) within the first block after the bridge.

WASHINGTON CROSSING INN. Also on the Pennsylvania side, this country inn has a large restaurant with several dining rooms, offering classic American cuisine. It is located at the corner of Routes 532 and 32.

SOFIA CAFÉ & RESTAURANT. This restaurant is on Route 31 in the little town of Pennington. Go east on CR 546 (Washington Crossing–Pennington Road) and then take Route 31 north.

BURGER KING. The nearest BK is in the Pennington Market shopping center, which is on Route 31 a few miles north of CR 546.

Nelson House.

19

Cooper River Park

COUNTY: Camden

TOWNS: Camden, Cherry Hill

TYPE: loop

RIDE DISTANCE: 10 miles

SURFACE: pavement

USAGE: Young Biker, Preschooler, Toddler

RIDE SUMMARY

Tucked deep in the neighborhoods of Camden County, three parks combine for some excellent biking. Cooper River Park, Maria B. Greenwald Memorial Park, and Challenge Grove have a network of paved bike paths linking the three parks. Along Cooper River through open and wooded areas, this trail system is a nice choice throughout the year, although there are two hazards. First, on the north side of Cooper River Park the path runs very close to the road, creating a safety problem for junior bikers. The second hazard is playgrounds! There are several top-notch play areas that can seriously slow down a family ride. Each playground has a restroom. Porta-potties are here and there.

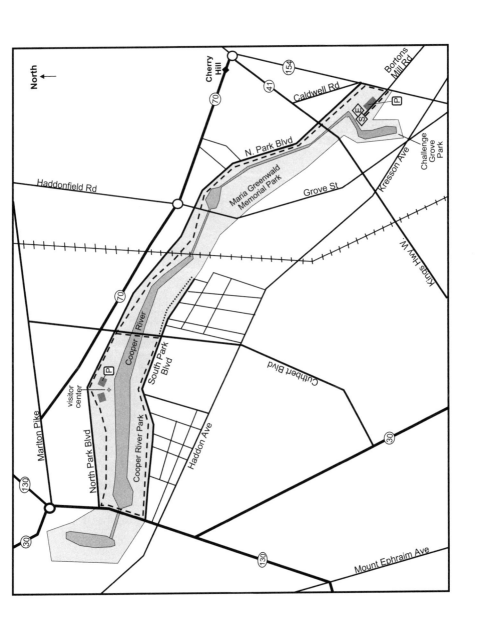

North

Cherry Hill

70

154

41

Bortons Mill Rd

Caldwell Rd

N. Park Blvd

Haddonfield Rd

Maria Greenwald Memorial Park

Grove St

Kresson Ave

Challenge Grove Park

Kings Hwy W.

P

Cooper River

70

South Park Blvd

Cuthbert Blvd

visitor center

P

Cooper River Park

North Park Blvd

Haddon Ave

30

Marlton Pike

130

30

130

Mount Ephraim Ave

RIDE DETAIL

Part of the Camden County park system, Cooper River Park at just over 340 acres encompasses a large section of Cooper River. The western border of the park is Route 130 and the eastern border is Grove Street. Immediately adjacent to Cooper River Park is the Maria Barnaby Greenwald Memorial Park, which, in turn, is adjacent to Challenge Grove Park. With three parks and multiple parking lots, there are many options for bike rides. For trail updates and park event schedules, go to the Camden County website at www.co.camden.nj.us.

PARK-PARK-PARK. For a long ride, using all three parks, begin at the southern end in Challenge Grove. Go southeast for a block, toward Route 154, and then follow the trail to North Park Boulevard. From here ride through the Greenwald Memorial Park, where there are a few dips and curves, to Grove Street. To access the trail system in Cooper River Park, cross Grove Street and follow the trail under the railroad tracks. From Cuthbert Boulevard, you can do a loop going further west on North Park and returning east on South Park. Cross back over the river on Cuthbert Boulevard and finish your ride back at Challenge Grove Park. This roundtrip is about 10 miles. There are restrooms and a nice picnic area at Challenge Grove. Restrooms are also available at the Cooper River Park visitor center. Porta-potties are near the parking lots.

COOPER PARK LOOP. For a nice, easy 3.8-mile loop, start at the main parking area near the visitor center in Cooper River Park. Go west on North Park, east on South Park and then back west on North Park. This loop takes you past the park's main features, including the playground, pagoda, miniature golf, and memorials. For a short extension of a mile or so, before crossing the river on Cuthbert Boulevard, continue east till the trail ends at Saginaw Avenue. There are restrooms at the visitor center and picnic tables near most parking areas.

ALTERNATE PARKING

To start your ride from Challenge Grove Park, take Exit 34 from I-295 to Route 70 West. Go south on Route 154 to Bortons Mill Road. Look for the park sign at the corner. The parking area stretches along the edge of the park.

WHERE TO START

To start your ride from Cooper River Park, take Exit 34 from I-295 to Route 70 West. Make a left onto Cuthbert Boulevard and then a right onto North Park Boulevard. The main parking area, near the visitor center, is a half mile further west. There are many other small parking areas around the park, including three on South Park Boulevard.

CAMDEN

This county park is a nice surprise. Just blocks from the Route 70 and 130 shopping centers, it supports a variety of activities with ball fields, a driving range, miniature golf, yacht club, cinder running track, picnic areas, and a boat launch. The park has also hosted several large rowing events, including the NCAA Women's National Rowing Championships and the U.S. Olympic Trials. Cooper River Lake has ideal rowing conditions with a world-class, Olympic-distance, 2,000-meter narrow and sheltered straightaway. With a smooth surface and very little wind, this stretch of the river often tempts rowing teams out to practice.

FOOD, FUN, AND RESTROOMS

Within a mile or so of the park there are both fast food and full-service restaurants. The following are only the closest and easiest to find.

LOBSTER TRAP. This full-service restaurant is in Cooper River Park on North Park Boulevard near the visitor center, main parking area, and track.

PARKWAY GOLF. Located right on North Park at the intersection of Cuthbert Boulevard, this miniature golf center also sells ice cream bars, soda, water, and juice.

BURGER KING. The closest BK is on Route 70. Take North Park east past Cuthbert Boulevard and make a left onto Delaware Avenue (a small side street). The BK is on the corner.

FRIENDLY'S. This restaurant is also on Route 70. Take North Park east past Cuthbert Boulevard and make a left onto Cornell Ave (a small side street). Friendly's is on the corner.

CAMDEN WATERFRONT. Cooper River Park is only 4 miles from the Camden Waterfront, which has great kids' stuff, including the Aquarium, a Children's Garden, and the Battleship New Jersey! To get there, take North Park west to Route 130 North. At the circle, take Route 30 (Admiral Wilson Blvd.) west to the exit for the Camden Waterfront/Mickle Boulevard/Martin Luther King Boulevard (one boulevard, two names). Bear right as it loops around and then continues west all the way to the Waterfront complex. From Route 30, 'A'quarium signs will also help to guide you. For more information, go to www.camdenwaterfront.com or call 856-757-9400.

New Jersey State Aquarium. With indoor and outdoor exhibits, the aquarium gets better every year and is a large part of the Camden Waterfront complex. The aquarium also houses the Riverview Café, which makes a good lunch stop, and there is a convenient parking garage next door. Admission is charged. For more information, go to www.njaquarium.org or call 856-365-3300.

Camden Children's Garden. Located on Riverside Drive, this is a 4-acre, interactive horticulture park, specially designed for children. For more information, go to www.camdenchildrensgarden.org or call 856-365-8733.

Battleship New Jersey. The nation's most decorated battleship is now a floating museum on the Delaware River. There is a guided tour lasting about two hours through the Iowa-class ship, one of the largest ever built. It is docked at Riverside Drive. For more information, go to www.battleshipnewjersey.org.

CHERRY HILL

FOOD, FUN, AND RESTROOMS

Challenge Grove is a wonderful little county park with clean rest-rooms, picnic tables, and a huge playground. Furthermore, within a few miles there are multiple fast food and full-service restaurants. Only a few of the choices that were within a mile of the intersection of Routes 70, 41, and 154 are listed here.

McDONALD'S. The nearest McD's is on Route 70 at the intersection of Routes 41 and 154. Take North Park east to Route 41 North.

PIZZA HUT. This eat-in pizzeria is in the shopping center just north of the intersection of Routes 70, 41, and 154.

CHILI'S. This restaurant is on Route 70, about a mile west of Route 41.

GARDEN STATE DISCOVERY MUSEUM. Geared for younger children, this hands-on museum offers fifteen larger-than-life, interactive exhibits and areas to explore, touch, and create in. It is open Tuesday–Sunday. Admission is charged. To find the museum, take Route 154 back to Route 70 and go east past I-295. Make a left onto Springdale Road. The museum is about a mile north. For more information, go to www.discoverymuseum.com.

COVERED BRIDGE. One of New Jersey's two covered bridges is located in Cherry Hill. This particular bridge over the Cooper River was designed by Bob Scarborough and constructed in 1959. To have a look, take Route 154 South and make a left (east) onto Kresson Avenue. Go about a mile, then make a left onto Covered Bridge Road (the last road before I-195). The bridge is about a mile north.

Pennsylvania Trails

New Hope canal boat ride.

20

Delaware Canal

COUNTIES: Northampton, Bucks

TOWNS: Riegelsville, Frenchtown, New Hope,
Washington Crossing Historic Park

TRAIL DISTANCES

Total Length 60 miles
Easton to Riegelsville 8.5 miles
Riegelsville to Black Eddy 7 miles
Blacky Eddy to Uhlerstown 3.5 miles
Uhlerstown to Lumberville 9 miles
Lumberville to Center Bridge 5 miles
Center Bridge to New Hope 1 mile
New Hope to Washington Crossing Historic Park 7 miles
Washington Crossing Historic Park to Bristol 19 miles

Constructed as part of a 1,200-mile network of canals to link
Philadelphia and Pittsburgh to Lake Erie, the Delaware Canal was
completed in 1834. The canal dropped 165 feet through twenty-
three locks, traversing 60 miles to connect Easton to Bristol. The
canal's primary purpose was the transportation of anthracite coal
from Pennsylvania to the major cities on the eastern seaboard. Other
goods, including lumber, stone, livestock, and agricultural products,
were also hauled on the canal, much of them used to sustain the

communities along its length. Today, the Delaware Canal is the only intact, continuous towpath remaining in America.

Conditions on the towpath vary from dirt single track, north of Riegelsville, to packed cinder from Lumberville south to Washington Crossing Historic Park and beyond. For much of its length, the towpath runs on the east side of the Delaware Canal forming an island in the Delaware River. Although this can make the rides long, since towpath access is limited to bridge crossings, it also provides long sections where the canal and towpath traverse fields and woods with no roads in sight. Access is further limited, particularly on the northern half, by parking limitations. If you cross into New Jersey, the bike path, following the D&R Feeder Canal and the Belvidere-Delaware Railroad, stretches from Milford to Trenton. For more information on creating a loop, refer to chapter 18, Delaware & Raritan Feeder Canal.

The majority of the trail is wide and very easy to ride. By using the towpaths on either side of the Delaware River, you can create any number of wonderful loops to suit your needs. I have detailed two rides: one on the northern half and the other on the southern half. Either can be extended, shortened, or turned into a loop. Just be careful when planning a trip south of Uhlerstown or north of Lumberville as the towpath runs 9 long miles through here without a break. In 2004, large sections of the towpath were destroyed by hurricane flooding. Check for current trail conditions at the Pennsylvania State Parks website under www.dcnr.state.pa.us/stateparks/ or call 610-982-5560.

RIEGELSVILLE TO FRENCHTOWN RIDE

COUNTY: Northampton
TOWNS: Riegelsville, Frenchtown
TYPE: out-and-back
RIDE DISTANCE: 21 miles
SURFACE: packed cinder
USAGE: Young Biker, Preschooler

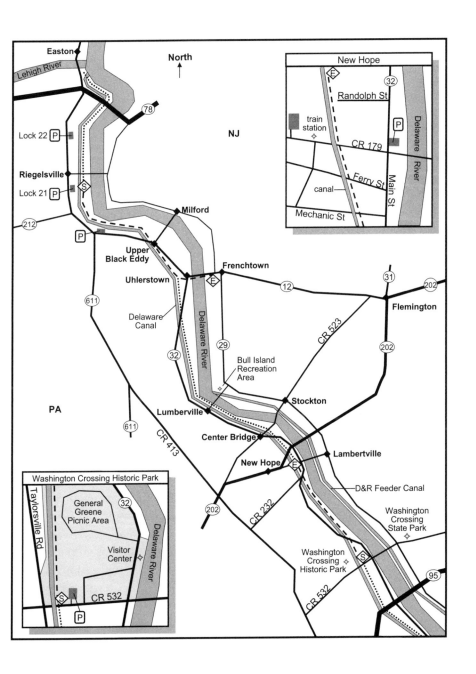

North

Easton

Lehigh River

78

NJ

Lock 22 P

Riegelsville

Lock 21 P S

Milford

212

P

Upper
Black Eddy

Frenchtown

Uhlerstown E

611

Delaware
Canal

32

Delaware River

12

31

202

Flemington

29

CR 523

202

Bull Island
Recreation
Area

PA

611

CR 413

Lumberville

Stockton

Center Bridge

Lambertville

New Hope E

202

CR 232

D&R Feeder Canal

Washington
Crossing
State Park

Washington
Crossing
Historic Park

CR 532

S

95

New Hope

E

Randolph St

32

train
station

P

CR 179

Delaware River

canal

Ferry St

Main St

Mechanic St

Washington Crossing Historic Park

Taylorsville Rd

General
Greene
Picnic Area

32

Visitor
Center

Delaware River

S

CR 532

P

RIDE SUMMARY

For a whole-day trip, the ride from Lock 21, just south of Riegels-ville, to Frenchtown is a great choice. While there is not much in Riegelsville, Frenchtown has a lot to offer and the scenery along the way is spectacular. The towpath surface begins as a dirt single track and changes to smooth packed cinder further south. The trail runs between the Delaware Canal and the Delaware River. There are no road crossings and long sections where even Route 32 is not visible. Restrooms and porta-potties are scarce.

RIDE DETAIL

The biking along the Delaware Canal is superb! Part of the allure is that there are no road crossings and the area around the canal is undeveloped, with many of the old houses and canal structures still standing. Riding down the "canal island" makes for a wonderful trip. Parking lots only appear every so often but there are several possible starting points. The first is at Lock 22–23. This is just south of Raubsville and makes the trip to Frenchtown and back almost 27 miles. The second is at Lock 21, where there are picnic areas and very nice restrooms. Lock 21 is a half mile south of Riegelsville. The third choice is at Kintnersville, near the intersection of Routes 611 and 32, which shortens the roundtrip to 15 miles. There is a picnic area here with access to the towpath.

We usually take the whole day to do this ride, so we start at Lock 21. The canal parallels the river and Route 611 for several miles and then diverges around Narrowsville. After the canal crosses under Route 32, it meanders through the countryside with only an occasional road crossing. If you want to cross to Milford at Upper Black Eddy, use Bridgeton Hill Road, but note that you cannot go north from Milford on the New Jersey side. Another 3.5 miles south is Uhlerstown. There are signs along the canal for Uhlerstown and, as in Upper Black Eddy, you must ride on the road a short distance. There are no houses on Uhlerstown Hill Road, so traffic is not an issue. The road intersects Route 32 about one block south of the

Canal picnic area.

bridge. Walk along the grass and cross Route 32 just before the bridge. On a busy weekend, this crossing can be difficult. Directly across the bridge is Frenchtown, where the restaurants and shops are all on Bridge Street.

WHERE TO START

From I-78, take Exit 75 and go south on Morgan Hill Road. At the first intersection, make a left (east) onto Cedarville Road. Within two miles, Cedarville Road goes back under I-78 and then intersects Route 611. Go south (right) on Route 611 through Raubsville and Riegelsville. Look for Lock 21 on your left just after Riegelsville.

ALTERNATE PARKING

If you want to ride north from Frenchtown, from I-287 take Route 202 south into Flemington. At the circle, take Route 12 west to Frenchtown. Make a left onto Bridge Street. The parking area is on the left just before the bridge to Pennsylvania.

WASHINGTON CROSSING HISTORIC PARK TO NEW HOPE RIDE

COUNTY: Bucks
TOWNS: Washington Crossing Historic Park, New Hope
TYPE: out-and-back
RIDE DISTANCE: 14 miles
SURFACE: packed cinder
USAGE: Young Biker, Junior Biker, Preschooler, Toddler

RIDE SUMMARY

Washington Crossing Historic Park, with its restored buildings, visitor center, displays, encampments, and picnic areas, makes a great base for this ride. From the far west side of the park off CR 532, it is about 7 miles north to New Hope, making the roundtrip about 14 miles. Throughout this section, the towpath has a smooth, packed cinder surface, and once in New Hope you can park your bikes at the Delaware Canal visitor center or continue through town on the towpath. The trip can also become a loop by returning on the D&R Feeder Canal towpath in New Jersey.

RIDE DETAIL

The southern end of the Delaware Canal is in Bristol, where the canal joins the Delaware River. Biking around the Philadelphia area, however, is not as nice as farther north. Once you get as far south as Morrisville, the canal moves away from the river and into an industrial area. Riding from Washington Crossing Historic Park allows you to use the picnic areas, restrooms, and playgrounds scattered throughout the park and to visit New Hope without worrying about parking. This is arguably one of the best bike trips, with historic sites, ice cream shops at both ends, and great restaurants and shops in New Hope for lunch and a break.

From the parking area on CR 532, ride north on the towpath. Within the first 2 miles, you cross Collingswood Road and then Route 32. From here north to the south side of New Hope, the towpath is between the canal and the Delaware River and there are very few roads or access points. At the southern end of New Hope, where CR 232 intersects Route 32, the canal is interrupted. Cross Route 32 into the Delaware Canal State Park parking area. There are restrooms here and it makes a great place to park bikes, allowing you to explore New Hope on foot. To continue on the towpath, cross the parking area and then the small white bridge over the canal where the New Hope Canal Boat rides begin. During the summer, you may see a canal boat and mules here. The towpath continues north through town, and the first several blocks provide a great place to practice yelling, "Low bridge!" like the canalers of the 1800s. Getting to street level from the towpath is possible at every road intersection but you will need to climb stairs. New Hope has lots of shops and restaurants but gets very crowded on weekends. Use the public parking lots to park your bikes and *walk* through town.

To make this ride a loop, cross the Delaware River into Lambertville, New Jersey. Once over the bridge, look for the canal immediately to the left. Go south on the New Jersey towpath to Washington Crossing State Park, whose facilities are on the opposite side of Route 29 (use the pedestrian bridge). For a longer loop, continue on the towpath through New Hope, north to Center Bridge, and cross the river into Stockton, New Jersey, before heading south again. This adds about 2 miles, making the roundtrip about 16 miles.

WHERE TO START

From I-95 in Pennsylvania, take exit 51. Follow Taylorsville Road north to CR 532. Go east (right) on CR 532 for about a block to the parking area on the left.

ALTERNATE PARKING

Starting a bike ride from New Hope is an adventure in itself. For a small town with a huge tourist draw, it is woefully short on parking near the canal and all the street parking is metered. If you really want to start here, use the public parking lots on the west side of town (take CR 179 west and look for signs). Walk back into town to access the canal.

FRENCHTOWN

One hundred years ago the population of Frenchtown was 1,545. Today, Frenchtown still has about the same number. This picturesque little town on the Delaware River is very similar to the village established in 1785 by Thomas Lowery, who built a gristmill and sawmill on the river. The area had several different names, including Sunbeam and Sherrod's Ferry, before the current name became permanent. "Frenchtown" came from a French-speaking immigrant, Mallet-Prevost, who settled in the area in the late 1700s.

The first small store in the town was a built around 1820. The first train came through town about 1853 on the Belvidere-Delaware Railroad line. The old railroad station, located next to the bridge, is now a café. For a very small town, there are a surprising number of choices for food, and most of the stores and restaurants are right on Bridge Street.

FOOD, FUN, AND RESTROOMS

BRIDGE STREET CAFÉ. This popular café on Bridge Street is across from the bridge and on the towpath. It is so popular with bikers that bike racks are provided.

FRENCHTOWN INN. This old, restored country inn is one block north of the bridge on Bridge Street and is a bit more formal than the other choices in town.

MARKET CAFÉ AND BAKERY. This café at the intersection of Routes 12 and 29 is also an ice cream shop.

FRENCHTOWN CAFÉ. This small restaurant serves breakfast and lunch and specializes in cappuccino and espresso.

GALASSO'S PIZZA. If pizza is the day's choice, this eat-in pizzeria is at the corner of Bridge Street and Route 29.

BUCK'S ICE CREAM & ESPRESSO BAR. If ice cream is what you are after, this shop is also on Bridge Street, one building north of the Route 29 turn.

RACE STREET CAFÉ. This casual restaurant is tucked into the corner, just off Bridge Street.

RIEGELSVILLE

Originally known as Shank's Ferry, this small town is part of Durham Township. When the Delaware Canal opened in 1832, Riegelsville, like many of the small villages along the Delaware River, enjoyed a small economic boom. Warehouses and factories were built along the canal to service the boats carrying coal, stone, iron, goods from the mills, and produce along the 60 miles from Easton to Bristol. As the canal declined, so too did Riegelsville until it became the quiet, peaceful town of today. This is a great area to find a country inn and settle back for a long lunch somewhere along your ride.

FOOD, FUN, AND RESTROOMS

BORDERLINE CAFÉ. This restaurant is located on Delaware Road between Route 611 and the canal.

RIEGELSVILLE INN. Built in 1838 by the town's founder, Benjamin Riegel, this historic stone inn has offered food and lodging to travelers for over 160 years. The Riegelsville Inn is open year-round for lunch, dinner, and Sunday brunch, with service in the dining rooms, on the enclosed second-floor porch overlooking the Delaware River, and in the pub. The inn is located on Delaware Road between the canal and the Delaware River.

INDIAN ROCK INN. This country inn was constructed in 1812 on a large bend in the Delaware River and tucked into the side of the mountain. The canal now passes between the river and road but there is a bridge to access the inn. With dining available in the Delaware Room, Canal Room, or on the porch, this inn has a casual atmosphere and a menu ranging from Mediterranean specialties to sandwiches. They also have a wide range of homemade desserts, which is probably why both my kids marked this as their favorite restaurant. The parking lot is large so bike parking is easy.

RAUBSVILLE INN. Three miles north on Route 611 in the little town of Raubsville, this eighteenth-century country inn has been renovated in the spirit of New Orleans and offers traditional cuisine to spicy Creole. Take Canal Road toward the river.

NEW HOPE

Beginning as a ferry crossing and continuing through the canal era, New Hope has deep roots in local history. Its name changed from Wells' Ferry to Canby's Ferry and by 1765 to Coryell's Ferry. The current name was established when the town gristmill, owned by Benjamin Parry, burned down. Parry also owned two mills in New Jersey, named the Hope Mill and the Prime Hope Mill. So when he rebuilt the mill around 1790, it became the New Hope Mill and the town name soon followed.

Not just a mill location or ferry crossing, New Hope was also an important stop on the York Road, as it was the halfway point between New York and Philadelphia. In the 1700s, a postal stage-coach left Philadelphia at 8 A.M. and arrived in New Hope around 6 P.M., with the horses being changed every 10 miles. Passengers typically stayed overnight at the Ferry Tavern (now known as the Logan Inn) or at the Lambertville Inn in New Jersey. The Delaware ferry continued operating until the early 1800s, when Parry and several financial backers obtained the ferry rights and constructed a covered wooden bridge across the river at a cost of $69,000. Completed in 1814, the toll bridge lasted until 1903, when a flood destroyed it. Not too long after the covered bridge was built, construction began on the Delaware Canal. Although not fully operational until 1834, the Delaware Canal generated even more traffic for the town. In its most productive years, just before and just after the Civil War, some three thousand mule-drawn boats traveled up and down the canal, moving over one million tons of coal across Pennsylvania every year. Today, the mule-drawn boats operating on the canal pull visitors, not coal, but the canal is still intact for the full 60 miles. A ride along a restored section of the canal or on the scenic railroad or a quiet lunch overlooking the Delaware River are just a few of the options this town offers. There are dozens of small shops, restaurants, and cafés as well as special events. For more information, go to www.newhopepennsylvania.com.

FOOD, FUN, AND RESTROOMS

ODETTE'S. Right on the canal overlooking the river, this restaurant is at the southern end of town, with a large parking area. It is open daily, serving lunch and dinner.

LOGAN INN. Established as a tavern in 1722, this is Buck County's oldest continuously operated inn. With classic cuisine served inside or on the patio, this restored eighteenth-century establishment is tempting. Located on South Main Street, it is open daily, serving lunch and dinner. There is some space behind the building for bike parking.

LULU'S CAFÉ. With a casual atmosphere and menu, this café offers a nice alternative to the more formal Logan Inn across the street. There is ample outdoor seating but no good place to park bikes.

BLUE TORTILLA. This restaurant offers Mexican fare in a casual atmosphere. It is on the northern end of town on Main Street. You may be able to park bikes in the public lot next door with no charge. Smile and ask nice?

STARBUCKS COFFEE SHOP. You cannot miss this one on the corner of Main Street at the bridge, right in the center of town.

GERENSER'S ICE CREAM. The local favorite for ice cream is on Main Street about a block south of the bridge.

THE LAST TEMPTATION. This is another option for ice cream, across the street from Lulu's Café. There is very limited indoor seating.

NEW HOPE CANAL BOAT RIDE. Located at the southern end of town at Lock 11, the one-hour, narrated mule-drawn canal boat ride is great fun. It operates afternoons from May through October, and a fee is charged. For more information, go to www.canalboats.com or call 215-862-0758.

NEW HOPE & IVYLAND RAILROAD. The train leaves New Hope six or seven times a day for a short ride behind Engine No. 40. It operates from May through November. For fares and schedules, go to www.newhoperailroad.com or call 215-862-2332.

WASHINGTON CROSSING HISTORIC PARK

Washington Crossing Historic Park actually has two sections: McConkey's Ferry and Thompson's Mill. Located 3 miles north on Route 32, Thompson's Mill includes several restored buildings, replicas of soldiers' huts, Bowman's Tower, and Bowman's Wildflower Preserve. McConkey's Ferry is on Route 32, immediately after the bridge. The visitor center, which houses a theater, exhibits, small gift shop, and restrooms, is located about one block north. A replica of Leutze's famous painting, *Washington Crossing the Delaware*, is on display. One of the best exhibits is at the Durham Boat House, which has replicas of the boats used by the army to cross the river. Other

Hessian soldier encampment.

buildings are open to the public but some charge a fee for the tour. The park also hosts special events throughout the year, including encampments, craft fairs, and demonstrations of colonial chores.

FOOD, FUN, AND RESTROOMS

TAYLORSVILLE STORE. This small store has a variety of gifts, snacks, ice cream, and cold drinks. It is on Washington Crossing Road (CR 532) within the first block after the bridge.

WASHINGTON CROSSING INN. This country inn has a large restaurant with several dining rooms, offering classic American cuisine. It is located at the corner of Routes 532 and 32.

DOMINICK'S PIZZA. This eat-in pizzeria is about two blocks north on CR 532 in a small strip mall at the intersection with General Sullivan Road.

GENERAL GREENE PICNIC AREA. This is up Route 32 just a bit. (The stone entrance is visible from the north side of the visitor center.) It includes several picnic areas and has restrooms. There are also multiple parking lots scattered around the loop.

BOWMAN'S HILL TOWER. The 110-foot tower was constructed in 1930 to commemorate this important lookout site. It is located in the Thompson's Mill section of the park. Admission is charged.

BOWMAN'S WILDFLOWER PRESERVE. This 100-acre wildflower preserve is in the Thompson's Mill section of the park, north of Bowman's Tower. Admission is charged.

21

Tyler State Park

COUNTY: Bucks

TOWN: Newtown

TYPE: loop

RIDE DISTANCE: 10 miles

SURFACE: pavement

USAGE: Young Biker, Preschooler, Toddler

RIDE SUMMARY

Tyler State Park offers miles of paved bike trails, looping through-out the park. The trail system is extensive and you can ride around the park edge or do smaller loops in the center. Beware, though—this park covers the Neshaminy Creek valley and many of the trails have a steep incline. The general rule is, as you ride away from the creek, you are going uphill. It was also incredibly crowded when we rode here, especially near the boathouse and causeway dam. There are separate trails for equestrians and several trails are not open to bikes so please read the signs as you go. The path was over 10 feet across and very smooth asphalt.

RIDE DETAIL

Opened in 1974, the park was originally a farm owned by George and Stella Tyler. The couple purchased the land in the early 1900s

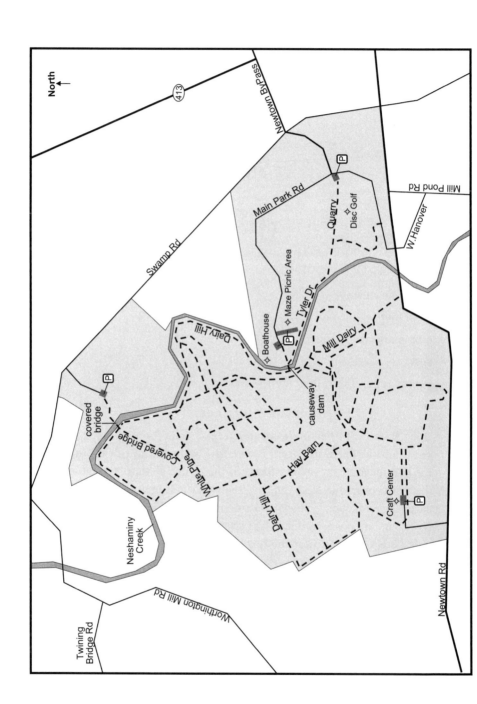

North

413

Newtown ByPass

Main Park Rd

Swamp Rd

P
Quarry
Disc Golf

Mill Pond Rd

W. Hanover

Maze Picnic Area

Tyler Dr

Boathouse

P

Mill Dairy

Dairy Hill

causeway
dam

P
covered
bridge

Covered Bridge

White Pine

Hay Barn

Dairy Hill

Craft Center
P

Neshaminy
Creek

Worthington Mill Rd

Twining
Bridge Rd

Newtown Rd

and used the Solly House as their country home until the mansion was constructed. The Tylers raised one of the finest Ayrshire dairy herds in the country. The stable housed their riding horses and the productive cropland was used to feed their livestock, which included poultry, sheep, and pigs. The existing stone buildings in the park are excellent examples of Pennsylvania farm dwellings from this period; some date all the way back to the early 1700s. Another notable structure in the park is the Schofield Ford Covered Bridge, the longest covered bridge in Bucks County. In 1991 this treasured landmark burned but by 1997 local volunteers, using authentic materials and methods, managed to rebuild the bridge on its original 1874 stone abutments.

Today, the facilities in this park make for a great day out. There are five different picnic areas, all with picnic tables, restrooms, drinking water, and connections to the park trail system. The Maze Picnic Area has a miniature barn, maze, and sandbox, while the adjacent area has a large playground. There is a 27-hole disc golf course, which begins at the first picnic area. Course maps with rules and scorecards are available at the park office. From Memorial Day to Labor Day, canoe rentals are available daily at the boathouse. Neshaminy Creek offers calm, easy boating upstream from the causeway dam. Two major craft fairs are also held in the park each year. With over 250 crafters, the first is on Memorial Day weekend and the second is in mid-October.

Tyler State Park spreads out over 1,700 acres in Bucks County. Neshaminy Creek meanders through the middle of the park, with most of the biking trails on the west side. There are 10.5 miles of bike trails, 4 miles of gravel hiking trails, and 9 miles of bridle trails.

Tyler Drive, the main trail on the east side of Neshaminy Creek, is easy to access from the very end of the Maze Picnic Area parking lot or from the causeway dam. Once you are on the west side of Neshaminy Creek, the Dairy Hill Trail goes north and south. To the north, the trail climbs uphill, while to the south, the trail meanders a few yards, then goes uphill. Yes indeed, all the trails go up! Not steeply enough to make you want to walk, but up nonetheless. The

Where did that turtle go?

park encompasses a valley around Neshaminy Creek so a good portion of the trails run either uphill or downhill. We did a very nice loop around the outside by making a left turn at every intersection after we passed the covered bridge. It is also possible to do a figure eight through the middle using the Dairy Hill, Hay Barn, and Mill Dairy trails. The trails are all marked at the intersections so it is not hard to stay oriented.

It was necessary to caution the kids on their speed coming down a few hills. A wipe-out on packed cinder is nasty but a wipe-out at 15 miles per hour on asphalt is beyond description and most first aid kits! We also reviewed the rules for passing horses since this is a very popular equestrian riding area. There were picnic tables and benches scattered about for rest stops but no porta-potties on the trail system. Along the creek, most of the trails were in the woods but about half the trails in this park are around fields. For current trail information, go to the Pennsylvania State Parks website under www.dcnr.state.pa.us/stateparks/ or call 215-968-2021.

WHERE TO START

From I-95 in Pennsylvania, take Exit 49 and go west on Route 332. Routes 413, 332, and finally 532 all merge to form the Newtown Bypass. The park entrance is on the left and well marked. Take the main park road down the hill to the boathouse and dam area, where there are two parking lots. The boathouse parking area has space for about thirty cars and provides the closest access to the causeway dam. The Maze Picnic Area is a quarter mile back and quite large.

ALTERNATE PARKING

For maximum biking distance, use the parking lot near the disc golf course. This is the first parking area and is at the beginning of the Quarry Trail. From this lot, use the Quarry Trail to go downhill to Tyler Drive, which takes you along the creek (on the only flat trail in the park) to the causeway dam.

Food, Fun, and Restrooms

In addition to the facilities in Tyler State Park, there are lots of choices in the vicinity for food, shopping, and exploring.

APPLEBEE'S, WENDY'S, AND PIZZA HUT. These are all within a quarter mile of the park entrance. Exit the park straight onto the Newtown Bypass/413 North, then make a right into the shopping center, where you will find these and several other options as well.

PEDDLER'S VILLAGE. A visit to this country village with over seventy specialty shops and six restaurants is the perfect complement to a day's biking. Located in Lahaska, Peddler's Village has a mix of jewelry, clothing, collectible, toy, and home-furnishing stores. Lahaska is about 11 miles north of Newtown; take Route 413 North and make a right (north) on Route 202. The restaurant selection there ranges from Jenny's Bistro to the Painted Pony Café, which is in the Giggleberry Fair complex, housing a grand carousel, the three-story play land known as Giggleberry Mountain, a game room, and much more. Other choices include the Cock 'n Bull, Peddler's Pub, and Spotted Hog.

22

Hugh Moore Park

COUNTY: Northampton

TOWN: Easton

TYPE: out-and-back

RIDE DISTANCE: 7 miles

SURFACE: pavement

USAGE: Young Biker, Junior Biker, Preschooler, Toddler

RIDE SUMMARY

Want to get your kids hooked on bike riding? Start with this trail. It is wide, paved, and level, with some sections through the woods and others in the open along the canal. A trip to the end of Hugh Moore Park can include a short ride on a restored barge pulled by mules and a visit to a locktender's house. If that does not work, there is a small playground, picnic areas, a dam on the Lehigh River, and a fish bypass on the Delaware River. You will also find restrooms in Hugh Moore Park and a porta-potty at the parking area on Route 611.

RIDE DETAIL

In 1962 the City of Easton purchased a 6-mile section of the canal south of Easton, along the Lehigh River. Hugh Moore, founder of the Dixie Cup Company, provided the funds. Eventually, these 260

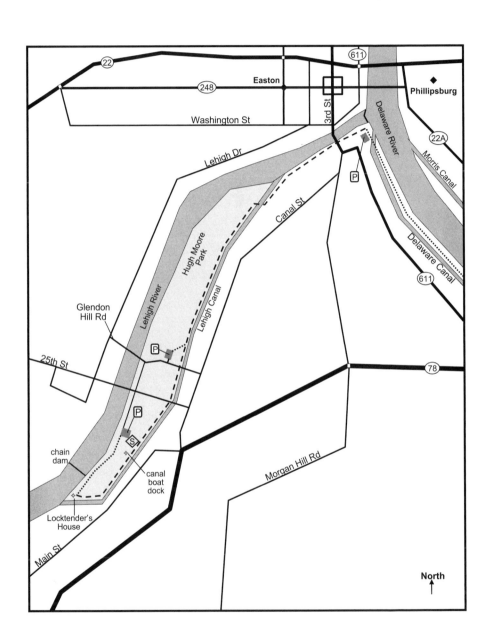

acres became Hugh Moore Park. It is devoted to preserving and interpreting America's canal and industrial revolution eras and includes a 2.5-mile section of restored canal with three operable locks, canal structures, and a locktender's house. With the mule-drawn canal boats and workers in period dress, a visit to this park is truly a trip back in time. There are picnic areas along the Lehigh River and a large playground located near the Canal Boat Store (open May through September).

The 3.5-mile bike path runs through Hugh Moore Park, which is operated and maintained by the National Canal Museum, to downtown Easton. The trail parallels or shares the Lehigh Canal towpath. It is easy to access from the main parking area and there are very nice restrooms here due to the canal boat ride. It is a very smooth pavement and one of only a few trails we have found that is suitable for very young toddlers. It is also a good choice for early spring or after rain. The area around the canal boat ride and locktender's house can be busy on weekends but the trail north toward Easton is generally quiet.

One of our favorite rides starts at the parking area in Easton and follows the paved path south through Hugh Moore Park. At Glendon Hill Road, we switch to the towpath for the ride to the locktender's house, at the far end of the canal island. For the return trip north, we take the paved path through the woods, then finish the ride back to Glendon Hill Road on the park road. As you travel through the park, you cannot miss the picnic area, playground, and canal boat ride, which I highly recommend. It is a great opportunity to put your feet up and let the mules do the work for a while! The round-trip from Easton is about 7 miles. For park information, check with the National Canal Museum at www.canals.org or call 610-515-8000.

For junior bikers, even those using training wheels, start in the main parking lot, go south to the locktender's house on the canal towpath, and return on the bike path through the woods. There are a couple of gentle slopes that might require walking the bike (or a slight push) but overall this is a nice, short ride to get your little one started on his/her own bike.

For a full-day or longer ride, start from the Hugh Moore parking lot and ride the towpath north to Easton. At the Route 611 parking area, the Lehigh River intersects the Delaware River. This is also the start of the Delaware Canal, which can be used to extend your ride. Be aware that the surface is a worn, rocky single track, and the upper Delaware Canal also has unusual geese. They look like normal geese but the feathered fiends do not move out of the way! Between the geese and the rough surface, travel on the upper part of the Delaware Canal is time-consuming. But for the brave, adventurous souls out there, traveling south on the towpath, you will get to Northampton County Park, which has a picnic area and playground, after 2 miles or so and Lock 22–23, which has a large parking area with picnic tables and restrooms, is another 4 miles south. The small town of Riegelsville is a very long 9 miles south. Before planning a trip extension on the Delaware Canal, go to www.dcnr. state. pa.us/stateparks/ or call 610-982-5560 for current conditions.

WHERE TO START

From I-78 in Pennsylvania, take Exit 75 and follow the signs for Route 611. From downtown Easton, take Route 611 South. Right in the middle of the curve after the Third Street Bridge, there is a gravel parking lot on the right.

ALTERNATE PARKING

If you want to start in Hugh Moore Park, from Route 611 in Easton take Canal Street south about 2 miles and go past the park exit. Continue on Canal Street to 25th Street. Make a right onto the 25th Street Bridge and immediately after the bridge, make a left onto Lehigh Drive. Continue around the loop and turn onto Glendon Hill Road, where you will find the park entrance. Once in Hugh Moore Park, make a right turn after you cross the Lehigh River bridge and follow the park road south to the main parking area. It is not really complicated—just follow the signs for the canal park.

It is also possible to park closer to the entrance to Hugh Moore Park. After you cross the Lehigh River bridge and just before the canal bridge, make a left turn into the gravel parking lot, which has space for about twenty or more cars. There is a restroom here but it is a bit crude. Parking here reduces the roundtrip ride to about 6 miles.

EASTON

Easton was founded in 1752 by Thomas Penn, the son of Pennsylvania's original proprietor, William Penn. Easton, named after Thomas Penn's father-in-law's estate in England, was laid out with the same concept used in Philadelphia—a grid around a "great square." It was in the Centre Square on July 8, 1776, that the citizens of Easton heard a public reading of the Declaration of Independence. This gives Easton the distinction of being one of only three colonial cities in which this important document was read publicly. During the Revolutionary War, Easton became a major supply center for the Continental Army and was used by General Sullivan to attack the Iroquois Indians who were allies of the British. In the nineteenth century, Easton became an early industrial center due to the conjunction of two rivers, three canals, and five railroads. Today, downtown Easton has lots to offer and is definitely worth investigating for both food and fun! Parking is not typically an issue. Look for the parking garage behind Two Rivers Landing.

FOOD, FUN, AND RESTROOMS

PURPLE COW CREAMERY. This little ice cream shop is located on South Bank Street, which is a walkway from the parking garage into the square.

McDONALD'S. There is a McD's in the Crayola Factory at Two Rivers Landing on Centre Square. And there is another McDonald's at the corner of Third Street and Washington Boulevard.

SUBWAY. Limited indoor seating is available at this Subway, located just off the Square.

PEARLY BAKER'S ALE HOUSE. This full-service restaurant is located on Centre Square. It is a favorite with local families; the staff is very good with kids.

Josiah White II.

PERKINS. This family restaurant is across from the Third Street Bridge.

NATIONAL CANAL MUSEUM. Take a journey back in time to the early 1800s and through interactive exhibits explore what life on the canals was like. Investigate the living quarters of a canal boat, listen to life-size figures recount tales and sing songs of canal life, and operate a model to pilot a boat though a lock. The museum is located at Two Rivers Landing on Centre Square. For more information, go to www.canals.org or call 610-515-8000.

CANAL BOAT RIDE. The mule-drawn canal boat *Josiah White II* offers a leisurely ride on Section 8 of the restored canal in Hugh Moore Park. The narrated ride takes thirty minutes or so and is operated from early May to late September. Tickets can be purchased at the Canal Boat Store.

LOCKTENDER'S HOUSE. Situated at the end of Section 8, this house is now a living history museum depicting the life of a locktender and his family. The house was constructed in 1920 as a residence for the family that operated Guard Lock No. 8. The canal boat ride ticket or entry fee to the National Canal Museum includes a pass to explore this house.

CRAYOLA FACTORY. Discover how crayons and markers are made while exploring more than a dozen interactive exhibits, with projects and activities for every age. The Crayola Factory is located at Two Rivers Landing on Centre Square. Closed most Mondays. For more information, go to www.crayola.com or call 610-515-8000.

23

Lehigh Canal

COUNTY: Northampton

TOWNS: Allentown, Bethlehem

TYPE: out-and-back

RIDE DISTANCE: 14 miles

SURFACE: packed cinder, dirt double track

USAGE: Young Biker, Junior Biker, Preschooler

RIDE SUMMARY

The Lehigh Canal towpath makes a great ride that is sure to become one of your favorites. Truly a "greenway," this trail is a huge surprise. It runs along between the canal and the Lehigh River, hidden among the trees through a largely industrial area. It is an easy ride from Freemansburg or Allentown with Bethlehem in the middle for food and fun. The only caution on this ride is the limited trail access. Due to the railroad tracks, there are very few. On an alternating surface of packed gravel or dirt double track, it is 7 miles from Canal Park in Allentown to the parking area in Freemansburg, making the roundtrip 14 miles.

RIDE DETAIL

The Lehigh Canal was constructed to carry anthracite coal from the upper Lehigh Valley to Easton. By 1825, over thirty thousand tons

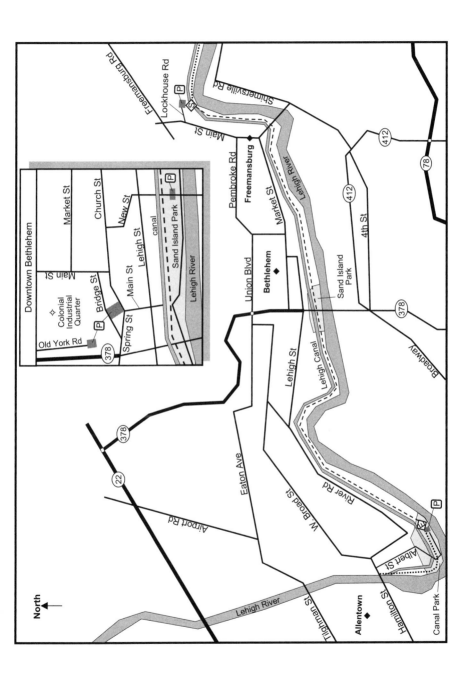

North

Downtown Bethlehem

Market St
Church St
New St
Lehigh St
Main St
Bridge St
Spring St
Old York Rd
378
Colonial Industrial Quarter
canal
Sand Island Park
Lehigh River
Main St

Freemansburg Rd
Lockhouse Rd
P
Main St
Shimersville Rd
412
78
Pembroke Rd
Freemansburg
Market St
Lehigh River
412
4th St
Union Blvd
Bethlehem
Sand Island Park
378
Broadway
Lehigh St
Lehigh Canal
Eaton Ave
378
22
Airport Rd
W. Broad St
River Rd
P
Albert St
Lehigh River
Tilghman St
Allentown
Hamilton St
Canal Park

of anthracite was literally floating down the river to Philadelphia annually. This navigation system was possible due to Josiah White's invention of hydrostatic locks, which increased the river depth by creating small artificial floods. Increased competition and a desire for both ascending and descending navigation led the company to rebuild its waterway into a conventional canal with lift locks by 1829. The enlarged Lehigh Navigation was over 46 miles running between Mauch Chunk (Jim Thorpe) and Easton. It had a total of 52 locks, 8 guard locks, 8 dams and 6 aqueducts enabling the waterway to overcome an elevation difference of almost 355 feet. The towpath was 8–10 feet wide and average speed was 2–3 mph with a two-mule draft. Life on a canal boat was a family business with wives and children working 15–20 hour days along-side boatmen, eking out a meager existence with "the company." A typical day started before 4 A.M. with the grooming and harnessing of the mule-team and ended at 10:00 P.M. or later when the locks stopped operating and the boats could go no further. A mule-powered boat loaded with 80 tons of cargo traveled 30 miles or more each day.

Despite the encroaching railroads, the Lehigh Canal system survived into the mid-1900s, when it was purchased by the state. Though the canal is not intact, new sections are opened for recreational use every year and the 7-mile section from Freemansburg to Allentown is a very nice ride. Coming from New Jersey, we usually elect to travel from east to west but the ride works just as well from west to east. Although the Freemansburg parking area is small, space is not usually an issue. If it is, use the parking area several blocks south at the base of Monroe Street. At the Lockhouse Road parking area, the canal is grass to the east, although the towpath continues. Follow the water southwest! The first mile or so takes you past the small streets of Freemansburg. Where the towpath turns west, the run to Sand Island Park is about 2 miles, through which the railroad tracks parallel the towpath and canal on the left while the Lehigh River is on the right. Sand Island is a Bethlehem municipal park at the base of Main Street. Encompassing the towpath, canal, and a section of river frontage, this park has picnic areas, tennis and basketball counts, restrooms, and a playground. An interesting aqueduct carries the canal over the Monocacy Creek, which enters the Lehigh River at the base of Sand Island. In the middle of the park near the Ice House, Lock 42 is partially restored and serves as a dam to keep water in the canal.

If you want to visit the historic sites or get a bite to eat, it is a very short distance to Bethlehem's historic downtown. Go north two short blocks along Main Street to Spring Street. The Colonial Industrial Quarter parking area is caddy corner to Main Street. Cross the Industrial Quarter parking lot to the base of Bridge Street, which is truly a bridge, where there is a trail to the Moravian Village and a path up to the downtown historic district. The majority of the restaurants and shops are on Main Street. We usually park our bikes near the base of Bridge Street and explore on foot.

Back on the towpath, if you reverse course here, it is 6 miles roundtrip. If you choose to keep going, the towpath continues on its way to Allentown from the west side of Sand Island Park near the boat rental. The canal and trail area are very wide all the way to Lock 41, after which there is more tree cover and less ground around the trail. Lock 41 has a small bridge over the canal and this lock was also converted into a small dam to help maintain the water level. The next section is mostly dirt double track and this is where the railroad appears. Although the tracks are never very far away on this ride, towards Allentown the canal and towpath go past the rail freight yard. The towpath passes "the hump," a gravity incline used by the railroad to roll (yup, literally *roll*) freight cars to the correct track in the freight yard. This process of "sorting" freight cars is fascinating to watch but the screeching brakes are loud. A little further on are the remnants of a water overflow, which allowed excess water to flow out of the canal into the river. It is marked by a depression and a few remaining stones still embedded in the towpath. After 4 miles, you reach Canal Park in Allentown. The gravel parking area is at the end of the park road. If you turn back from this parking area, your roundtrip from Freemansburg is about 14 miles. Unfortunately, neither end has restrooms or porta-potties. If you need a pit stop, do not miss the restrooms in Sand Island Park.

It is possible to continue biking for another half mile or so through Canal Park on the park road or on the towpath, but the area is not as nice. You can continue past Lock 40, which again functions as a dam, under the railroad bridge to Hamilton Street, making your roundtrip from Freemansburg closer to 16 miles.

WHERE TO START

From I-78 in Pennsylvania, take Exit 67. Go north on Route 412 for a mile and make a right onto Shimersville Road. Go another mile and make a left onto Main Street, which takes you over the Lehigh River into downtown Freemansburg. Lockhouse Road is a half mile north, just before the railroad bridge, and the parking area has space for five cars.

ALTERNATE PARKING

If the Lockhouse Road lot is full, there is a larger lot at the end of Monroe Street, which has a red wooden bridge over the canal. Starting here does not significantly change your mileage.

It is easy to split this ride by starting from Bethlehem. If you ride west to Allentown, the roundtrip is 8 miles. If you ride east to Freemansburg, the roundtrip is 6 miles. Use the parking areas in Sand Island Park. There are several lots to the east of the Main Street entrance, which is also where the restrooms are located. If the east-side parking areas are full, go west toward the boat rental, which has an absolutely huge parking lot.

If you want to ride from Allentown, take Route 145 south from Route 22. A couple of miles south, make a left (east) onto Hamilton Street. Immediately after crossing the Lehigh River, make a right onto Albert Street and then another right onto Walnut Street. Follow the signs for Canal Park. The boat rental parking lot is at the far end of the park road.

BETHLEHEM

Freemansburg is where the ride begins but it is largely residential. It is Bethlehem that I recommend saving time to visit. The town of

Bethlehem has embraced its Moravian roots with a large restoration project right in the downtown district. Moravian Church missionaries settled in the area around 1741 and seven years later, with a population of 395, the town had thirty-eight industries. Today, the remnants of the once bustling village have been restored, along with the Burnside Plantation and Goundie House. While these historic sites are wonderful, save time to explore the downtown historic district. There are several blocks of restaurants and shops, all within walking distance.

FOOD, FUN, AND RESTROOMS

COLONIAL INDUSTRIAL QUARTER. The cornerstone of the Bethlehem historic district, this site highlights some fascinating pieces of Moravian history, including the 1761 Tannery, a dye house, and the 1762 Waterworks, a restored building from the nation's first municipal pumped water system. In the 1770s, this village had three pumps powered by waterwheels turned by the Monocacy Creek. Spring water was pumped up to the water tower, from which it flowed down to four cisterns at various locations in town. Then there is the 1869 Luckenbach Mill, housing HistoryWorks!, an interactive children's gallery. Self-guided walking tour brochures are available at the mill. The museum is open Saturdays through July and August. For more information, go to www.historicbethlehem.org.

GOUNDIE HOUSE. This Federal-style building was Bethlehem's first brick residence. Built in 1818 by John Goundie, a prominent Moravian brewer and community leader, it has been restored to its early nineteenth century appearance.

BURNSIDE PLANTATION. In 1748 James Burnside and his wife built a private residence on their 500-acre farm at the edge of the Moravian settlement. Considering that Moravians lived in communal houses for single men, single women, and married people, this was an unusual move for a Moravian missionary. Today, 7 acres of the original farm have been converted into a living history museum, interpreting farming between 1748 and 1848, a time of great change in agricultural methods.

Moravian Waterworks.

HEAVENLY HEDGEHOG. An ice cream shop located next to a toy store—what more could you want? The Main Street Commons is located at the end of Main Street, where it meets Broad Street. There is also a pizzeria on the lower level.

BETHLEHEM BREW WORKS. This full-service restaurant is on the corner of Main and Broad Streets in the Main Street Commons. Closed Monday and Tuesday.

CONFETTI CAFÉ. This café on Main Street has a light menu and also serves ice cream.

TORTILLA FLAT. This authentic Mexican restaurant is about midway up Main Street.

MORAVIAN BOOKSHOP AND DELI. Located across Main Street from the Colonial Industrial Quarter, this bookshop is also a deli and coffeehouse.

COLONNADE STEAKHOUSE. Want a more formal atmosphere? This steakhouse in the Radisson Hotel on Main Street should do it.

McDONALD'S. To reach the closest McD's, take Route 378 south over the Lehigh River and make a left (east) onto Route 412.

ALLENTOWN

William Allen was an eighteenth-century aristocrat as well as a successful colonial businessman and one-time mayor of Philadelphia. In 1762 he drew up plans for a village along the Lehigh River, which he named Northamptontown. Allen hoped the Lehigh River would help draw industry to the area but the low water level limited river trade. And so, through the Revolutionary War, "Allens town" remained a small village of Pennsylvania Dutch (actually, German) farmers. It was not until 1838 that the town officially adopted the name Allentown. The arrival of the Lehigh Canal and the railroads finally accomplished what William Allen had dreamed of—an industrial revolution. The 1850s saw the rise of a strong iron industry, which lasted until the Panic of 1873. In the twentieth century Allentown again boasted of a strong economy, with a much wider base that included silk mills, parlor furniture, beer, and cigars. In recent history, Allentown has transformed itself again to support the service industry, and the city has embarked on a downtown revitalization project. Unfortunately, biking into the downtown area is not yet feasible.

FOOD, FUN, AND RESTROOMS

BENNIGAN'S GRILL AND TAVERN. To find this family-friendly restaurant, take Route 145 south of Allentown and make a right onto Lehigh Street.

KING GEORGE INN. This restored eighteenth-century country inn is 4 miles west of the Lehigh River at the corner of Cedar Crest Boulevard and Hamilton Street.

O'HARA'S RESTAURANT AND PUB. This restaurant with a casual atmosphere is 4 miles west of the Lehigh River on Hamilton Street, just before I-78.

HAINES MILL MUSEUM. During colonial times, this mill operated on Cedar Creek. It is still functional today and demonstrations are given on weekend afternoons from May through September. Admission is free. To find the mill, go west on Hamilton Street, cross over Cedar Crest Boulevard, and make a right onto Haines Mill Road.

LENNI LENAPE HISTORICAL SOCIETY. This museum is dedicated to preserving the local Lenape (Delaware Indian) culture as well as educating the public on the original inhabitants of the Lehigh Valley. The Lenape were farmers, hunters, and fishermen, who had permanent settlements throughout the area, including the site of the museum. Displays include artifacts, cultural items, agricultural tools, and related natural materials as well as interactive exhibits for kids to explore and experience life as a pre-Colonial Lenape child. The museum also sponsors several annual Native American festivals. It is located in Little Lehigh Park. Take Hamilton Street west to Route 29 and go under I-78. Fish Hatchery Road is the second left. For more information, visit www.lenape.org.

24

McDade Trail

COUNTY: Monroe

TYPE: out-and-back

RIDE DISTANCE: 10 miles

SURFACE: packed gravel

USAGE: Young Biker, Preschooler

RIDE SUMMARY

The McDade Recreational Trail is being constructed in sections along the Pennsylvania side of the Delaware Water Gap National Recreation Area. The first 5 miles run from the Hialeah Picnic Area to Turn Farm. With the river, woods, and historic sites, this is an interesting ride but it is *not* flat. There are significant dips and climbs. In fact, the only flat area is around Smithfield Beach, which is also the only paved section, although most of the trail has a packed gravel surface that is easy to ride on. All the bridges are in great shape and there are no roads to cross except the canoe pickup area at the southern end of Smithfield Beach. There are restrooms at Smithfield Beach and porta-potties at both ends.

RIDE DETAIL

The Delaware Water Gap National Recreation Area is 70,000 acres, making it the largest recreation area in the eastern United States.

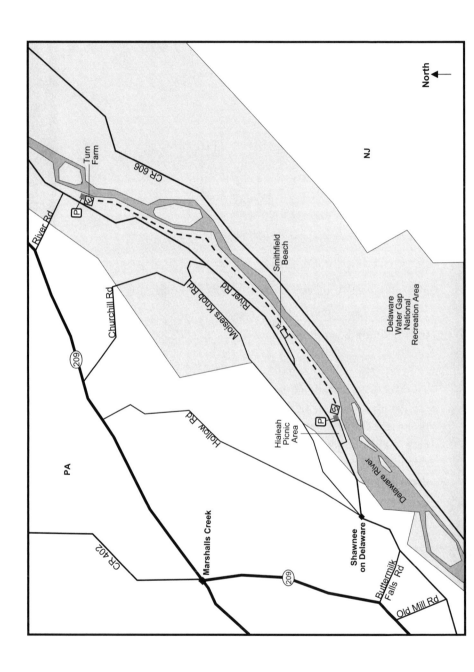

Originally conceived to help manage the Delaware River resources, it became a battle zone in 1960 when the Army Corps of Engineers launched a project to dam the river at Tocks Island, just north of the Gap, creating a 37-mile reservoir. For the next several decades, an area of serene farms, historic landmarks, individual homes, and small villages was systematically dismantled on both sides of the river. After years of hearings and meetings with locals, environmentalists, and geologists (all of whom fervently opposed the project), it was scrapped for good in 1992 and funding was finally provided to develop the park and preserve its few remaining historic landmarks.

The McDade Trail is one of these developments. Beginning at the Hialeah Picnic Area, the trail runs parallel to the Delaware River to Smithfield Beach and then on to Turn Farm. The packed gravel surface makes for easy riding but there are some surprisingly steep hills. Just north of Hialeah in the first mile or so are some of the steepest (mountain-sized, and induced so many groans I quit counting!). There are more hilly sections as you approach Turn Farm. Although the hills are difficult, the biggest hazard on this trail is poison ivy! The green leafy creeper is everywhere along the edges of this trail. Be wary of wandering about on foot. Remember, three leaves and shiny—leave it be.

At the Hialeah Picnic Area, the trail is easy to find at the north end, where there is a gravel parking area. From Hialeah to Smithfield Beach is about 1.5 miles. Through the beach area, where the trail runs quite conveniently past both restrooms, the path was paved. The next landmark, Flying Hawks Model Air Field, is visible across the field a mile or so north. Along the remaining 2.5 miles, the trail winds alongside fields and through woods and eventually ends at Turn Farm, where there are a few remnant farm buildings. Turning back here makes the roundtrip about 10 miles. For current trail information, go to the National Park Service website at www.nps.gov/dewa/.

WHERE TO START

From I-80 in Pennsylvania, take Exit 309. Follow Route 209 north for a mile or so and then turn right onto Buttermilk Falls Road. At

River Road, make a left (north). The Hialeah Picnic Area is just over two miles north on your right.

ALTERNATE PARKING

If you want to start at Turn Farm, continue on Route 209 through Marshalls Creek toward Bushkill. Make a right onto River Road and continue into the recreation area. The Turn Farm parking area is on the left within a mile of Route 209.

FOOD, FUN, AND RESTROOMS

While facilities in the recreation area are still scarce, the surrounding area, from Stroudsburg to Bushkill, provides lots of choices.

Poison ivy.

SHAWNEE GENERAL STORE. Located in the quaint village of Shawnee on Delaware, on the corner of Hollow and River Roads, this small country store has a little bit of everything.

BUSHKILL FALLS. A longstanding treasure of the Poconos, Bushkill Falls has a variety of hiking trails beside the river and waterfalls plus a gift shop, ice cream parlor, snack bar, and wildlife exhibit. Open daily from April to November. Admission is charged. For more information, go to www.visitbushkillfalls.com or call 570-588-6682.

POCONO BAZAAR AND FLEA MARKET. This large, longstanding flea market is open every weekend of the year from 9 A.M. to 5 P.M. With dozens of vendors, it attracts a huge crowd. Whether you are bargain hunting or just want to avoid the traffic jam, it is located on Route 209 at the intersection of Route 402 in Marshalls Creek. For more information, go to www.poconofleamarket.com.

DAIRY QUEEN. The DQ is easy to spot on Route 209 south of Marshalls Creek.

LANDMARK CAFÉ. This is a full-service, casual restaurant located on Route 209 south of Marshalls Creek.

MCDONALD'S. The closest McD's is in East Stroudsburg. Go south on Route 209 and then about a block before I-80, go east on Ridgeway Street. The McDonald's is about halfway down the block. If you are heading back into New Jersey, there is another McD's right off I-80 in Columbia, which is the first exit after the Gap.

AMERICAN CANDLE. Another Pocono tourist attraction, the American Candle Shop is on Route 611 just west of Stroudsburg. Follow Route 209 west and then take Route 611 North. For more information, go to www.american-candle.com.

CAMELBACK BEACH. This water park can be found in Tannersville, just 9 miles west on I-80. Perched on Camelback Mountain, the park offers a variety of fun water activities from wave pools to water slides. Open during the summer. Admission is charged. For more information, go to www.camelbeach.com.

Rejected Trails

While researching and exploring trails, we found several in New Jersey and one in Pennsylvania that were just not quite right. Sometimes we could not find the trail. Other times we felt that the trail conditions were substandard or unsuitable for children. And then there were a few trails that just had too much traffic.

DELAWARE WATER GAP—BLUE MOUNTAIN LAKES TRAIL. Much like the McDade Trail, this one goes up and down as it loops around Blue Mountain Lake and Hemlock Pond. The well-marked trail system is built on old roads, which have a pulverized stone surface. This long, 10-mile loop is just a little too much for my kids to be fun. Perhaps in another year or so? If you have a sturdy toddler and need some serious exercise, you might want to try this one. It is easy to find on the Delaware Water Gap maps.

PEQUEST TROUT HATCHERY. There are actually two rail-trails through this park in Warren County. The "lower" trail, which is visible from Route 46, has a ballast surface that is impossible to ride on. This is the right-of-way that runs through the trout hatchery grounds. The "upper" trail is an older rail-trail that runs from the intersection of Routes 31 and 46, just north of Oxford. From the gravel parking area, the trail goes over the river and runs about 1.5 miles to Pequest Road. There is a paved path just a bit to the west that runs another 1.5 miles into Oxford. I did not include this trail for two reasons. First, it is not a maintained trail and the puddles are already huge. Second, the path seems to be part of an extensive network of ATV and dirt bike trails.

ALLAMUCHY MOUNTAIN STATE PARK. This state park is just north of Hackettstown, in northern Warren County. The vast majority of trails are unsuitable for family biking. They are narrow, rocky, twisting, mostly unmarked, and present a wonderful challenge for hard-core mountain bikers.

HEDDEN PARK. This is a small Morris County park with one very short paved path suitable for biking. It takes longer to unload the bikes than to bike!

PATRIOTS' PATH. This is a network of trails throughout Morris County. The trail system is evolving and improving each year and the county is committed to its development. We explored several areas and discovered mostly mountain biking trails. The section we did find family-friendly is described in chapter 5.

LEWIS MORRIS PARK. This Morris County park has miles of trails— none suitable for family biking. We have tried multiple times to find flat, even sections and failed.

JOCKEY HOLLOW. This is a section of the Morristown National Historical Park in Morris County. Several trails within the Patriots' Path system run through the park but bikes are not allowed.

CHEESEQUAKE STATE PARK. This state park in Middlesex County lists both biking and mountain biking for its trail use. And there are definitely some very popular mountain biking trails. However, we never found "biking" trails. Most of the biking seems to be on the park roads. The rangers also seem pretty strict here as to which trails are open to bikes.

HENRY HUDSON TRAIL. This is a 9-mile rail-trail in Monmouth County that runs from Aberdeen to Atlantic Highlands on the old Central Railroad right-of-way. Unfortunately, this trail has eleven street crossings along the 9 miles. Many of these are smaller side streets but traffic is very heavy coming and going from Route 36. Even worse, several sections of the trail run parallel to Route 36, making for an unpleasant ride due to traffic noise.

NOTE: Monmouth County is extending this trail a further 9 miles. We have not yet explored the new section to Freehold.

ISLAND BEACH STATE PARK. This popular park in Ocean County has a designated bike trail running the length of the park. Unfortunately, the "path" is actually the two-foot-wide shoulder along the main park road. Because of the heavy traffic and the overgrown bushes we never unloaded the bikes. It's a great beach though!

SPRUCE RUN RECREATION AREA. This state park in Hunterdon County lists both biking and mountain biking for its trail use. However, all of the biking is on the park roads or along a very short section of paved path near the shore of the reservoir that is suitable for a young biker on training wheels or just getting started. Whereas this park charges a daily use fee during the summer, there are lots of free township parks with half-mile trails.

VOORHEES STATE PARK. The state park guide lists biking trails at this park in Hunterdon County. Unfortunately, as in many state parks, the bike trails are the access or loop road for the park.

ROUND VALLEY RECREATION AREA. Rather than use my words, I will borrow a description from a mountain biking enthusiast, "The terrain here compares to anything the Poconos have to offer. It's rough. It's tough. It's real mountain biking."

WASHINGTON VALLEY PARK. This 700-acre Somerset County park contains the former Bound Brook Elizabethtown Reservoir. The park has 7 miles of hiking and biking trails but only for mountain biking.

LEHIGH GORGE. This 25-mile rail-trail is easy riding all the way to Jim Thorpe, Pennsylvania. Unfortunately, it is 25 miles! There is only one other place to access the trail. Everyone we know either drops a car in Jim Thorpe or uses one of the shuttle services to get to the start. While the trail is wonderful and the scenery along the Lehigh River is gorgeous, all this trekking about is a bit much with kids. We rode north from Jim Thorpe one afternoon and got about 10 miles out before turning around.